Carr

Interpreting a Great Tradition

THE
LONDON CENTRE FOR
SPIRITUALITY

DISCARDED

The Church of St Edmund the King, Lombard Street EC3

My whole yearning was, and still is,
that as He has so few friends,
these should be good ones.

ST TERESA OF AVILA

Carmel

Interpreting a Great Tradition

Ruth Burrows

Dimension Books
Starrucca, PA 18462

Sheed & Ward
London

ISBN 0 87193 321 5 (U.S. edition)
ISBN 0 7220 1451 1 (U.K. edition)

Published in the United States of America by
Dimension Books Inc.
P.O. Box 9
Starrucca, PA 18462

and in the U.K. by
Sheed & Ward Ltd.
4 Rickett Street
London SW6 1RU

Edited, designed and typeset by Bill Ireson
Printed in Great Britain by
Biddles Ltd., Guildford and King's Lynn

Foreword

This book is written by a Carmelite who has a firm intellectual grasp of the charism and values of the Carmelite vocation. She writes with the authority of many years of lived experience of her own Carmelite community and I commend it without hesitation for its clarity, perception and conviction.

PETER SMITH
Bishop of East Anglia

Contents

CONTENTS

Preface

In her preface to *Living in Mystery*, Ruth Burrows wrote that she took courage from the words of John Paul II's *Orientale Lumen*:

> The men and women of today are asking us to show Christ, who knows the Father and has revealed him . . . we are called to show in word and deed today the immense riches that our churches preserve in the coffers of their tradition.[1]

She later speaks of her own vocation being based on the truth of the communion of saints and of the intimate spiritual bonding of us all and our mutual influence at the most spiritual, hidden level.

It is the living of that hidden level of the spiritual life in Carmel, preserved in the coffers of the Church's tradition, that Ruth Burrows now seeks to explain to a wider audience in the Church and beyond. The author needs no introduction, her writings have become spiritual classics of our time, drawing wisdom from scripture and the Carmelite saints. St Teresa of Avila's simple charter, 'Prayer is your business, such is the purpose of our life in Carmel', has been an inspiration. A lifetime of living this, for many years as prioress, ensures that she is now uniquely qualified to bring a fuller understanding of a great tradition to her readers.

The life of Carmel is still misunderstood by many, others are fascinated by it. The often phrased question, 'Why don't the sisters do some useful work as teachers, nurses, missionaries?' needs an answer. The book clearly does this, drawing on the same unwavering conviction that convinced St Thérèse of Lisieux that her work for souls lay within the silence and hidden life of Carmel. That hidden work goes on in the life of the Church, drawing some apart to watch daily at wisdom's door. Vatican II insisted[2] that they have a hidden apostolic fruitfulness and must be left in their solitude. From that solitude Ruth Burrows does us a great service by opening the treasures of such a great tradition hidden from many in the coffers of the Church.

ROGER SPENCER
Chaplain
Quidenham Carmel

CHAPTER ONE

Great Desires

When St Teresa of Avila determined to found a Carmelite monastery of strict observance faithful to the ideals of the Order, her aim was a life that positively expressed passionate devotion and commitment to God, and thereby opened those who embraced it to receive a passionate love for God. Passion in this context does not mean a state of heightened religious emotion, but an all-engrossing preoccupation with God, a most 'determined determination'[1] to give God all, to hold nothing back: 'the blessing of giving ourselves wholly to Him, and keeping nothing for ourselves'[2]. Over and over we hear it:

> This house is another Heaven, if it be possible to have Heaven on earth. Anyone whose sole pleasure lies in pleasing God and who cares nothing for her own pleasure, will find our life a very good one; if she wants anything more, she will lose everything, for there is nothing more she can have.[3]

Teresa constantly speaks of 'perfection', 'great perfection'. Aspirants to the Order 'must be persons of prayer desiring full perfection'[4]. She herself was determined to observe the Evangelical Counsels with 'all perfection' thus expressing her love for Christ, and was equally determined to ensure that her nuns did the same[5]. Imperfect

1

they might be and often were, but they must fix their desire on an all-consuming love for God; God 'loved above all things and with a passion that makes us entirely forget ourselves'.[6] Are they ready to pay the price for this love? If not, they should look elsewhere for a form of life that makes less demands.[7]

What has happened all too often, perhaps imperceptibly, is that the life-style has been adapted to non-passion. This is to betray not only the charism but those who, in good faith, entrust themselves to us in order to be taught and prepared for a great love of God. It is almost inevitable that a charism such as this will be received by others in varying measure and maybe only minimally. While the human source of it still lives and is able to inspire others, fervour will prevail, but as her influence fades, others less endowed, no doubt struggling to be faithful but lacking the inner vision, will concentrate more and more on preserving the letter of the constitutions, and even venerated small customs. But lacking an overall vision and, to a some extent the unifying centre, these disparate parts lie unconnected, meaningless, like spokes of an old wheel disengaged from the hub. Whatever the cause and nature of the decline, we are called to renewal and that entails a study of and re-creation of the original charism. Who can question that that charism is one of single-minded, radical, wholehearted God-centredness? Teresa herself was convinced that fidelity to the observance she had established, and unswerving steadfastness in prayer, would without doubt open her nuns to the closest union with God.

We read in the *Life*[8] that the idea of founding a reformed convent of the Carmelite Order was, to begin with, but a vague notion; only when another sister raised the possibility with some enthusiasm, did St Teresa begin to consider it seriously. Even then, as she tells us, she experienced no compelling urge but was content to remain where she was, in her pleasant convent. Nevertheless, the idea had, in fact, taken root and begun to grow. She herself was longing for greater seclusion. According to her own testimony, it was the Lord Himself who took the initiative, giving her the most explicit commands to found the convent and to work for this aim with all her might, making great and wonderful promises; that the convent would not fail to be established; that great service would be done to Him in it and that the convent would be a star giving the most brilliant light. Convinced she had received a divine mandate, and that here was an opportunity for expressing her love for Christ, her zeal gathered momentum, and the great trials she endured in founding the convent fuelled her passion.

As far as we can discern from St Teresa's writings, all she envisaged to begin with was a monastery of great perfection adhering faithfully to the Rule of the Order of Carmel – the Rule of St Albert, observing the strictest enclosure, founded on prayer and penance. Having been shown a copy of the Rule, she was enamoured. It embodied what her own soul, with its passion for prayer and craving for poverty, sorely needed:

> Oh, the greatness of God! I am often astounded when I think about this and realise how specially anxious His Majesty was to help me carry out the business of this little corner of God's house (for such, I believe, it is) and this dwelling in which His Majesty takes delight – once, when I was in prayer, He told me that this house was the paradise of His delight. So it seems that His Majesty had chosen the souls whom He has drawn to Himself and in whose company I am living, feeling very, very much ashamed of myself, for I could

never have expected to have souls like these for this plan of living in a state of strict enclosure and poverty and prayer.[9]

The foundation of this one house of 'great perfection' proved to be only a beginning. A powerful invasion of light and love was to impel Teresa to make many more foundations and what is of utmost significance, to enrich the charism, marking it indelibly with an apostolic character. Carmel is wholly apostolic.

Undoubtedly, there has always been implicit in the Church, an understanding that a life of contemplation of its very nature, benefited others, but for Teresa, the apostolic motive became 'the principle reason for which the Lord has brought us together in this house'.[10] She describes the occasion that opened her fully to this aspect of the vocation and urged her on, at enormous cost to herself and others, to make many more foundations. A Franciscan friar who had just returned from the Indies, came to see Teresa and talked to her and her nuns of the 'many millions of souls perishing there for lack of teaching . . . ' She continues:

> I was so distressed at the way all these souls were being lost that I could not contain myself. I went to one of the hermitages, weeping sorely, and called upon Our Lord, beseeching Him to find me a means of gaining some soul for His service . . . I begged Him that my prayer might be of some avail, since I had nothing else to give . . . While suffering this terrible distress, I was praying one night when Our Lord appeared to me in His usual way, and said to me very lovingly, as if He wished to bring me comfort: 'Wait a little while, daughter, and you will see great things.'[11]

From then on, the 'salvation of souls', praying for the Church and the prelates and theologians who defend her, was her ruling passion, identified with her love for Christ.

Over and over again, we hear her lamenting the state of the Church, of the 'havoc the Lutherans were making'. Teresa's zeal was not mere emotion: it led her to exhort and train her daughters in all perfection. Mediocrity was unthinkable; she insisted that they attend to even the smallest faults and failings, the motes, the particles, the little worms that gnaw away insidiously and destructively. The asceticism she insists on is every bit as searching, as absolute as that of John of the Cross and all for the sake of the 'great enterprise' – life dedicated to the welfare of the Church.

It is not uncommon for some to claim that the purely contemplative life was St Teresa's second choice. She was hindered by her sex and by her infirmities from being what we would call today an 'apostolic religious'. She can be quoted to this effect:

> . . . there came to my notice the harm and havoc that were being wrought in France by these Lutherans [she refers, of course, to the French Huguenots] and the way in which their unhappy sect was increasing. This troubled me very much, and, as though I could do anything, or be of any help in the matter, I wept before the Lord and entreated Him to remedy this great evil . . . And, seeing that I was a woman, and a sinner, and incapable of doing all I should like in the Lord's service, and as my whole yearning was, and still is, that, as He has so many enemies and so few friends, these last should be trusty ones, I determined to do the little that was in me – namely, to follow the evangelical counsels as perfectly as I could, and to see that the few nuns who are here should do the same.[12]

She expresses herself similarly in other places. But a full reading of her works as well as what she actually did, what her actual choices were, leave us beyond any doubt that these were but the emotional expressions of her love for our Lord and zeal for his Church. Far more frequently we find her extolling the privilege, the holiness, the fruitfulness of the enclosed, hidden life of her daughters. In their deep seclusion they were in the forefront of the fighting line. She assigns to them the office of standard bearer.[13] They wield no weapons, strike no blows, but remain passive, holding aloft the standard, prepared to be cut to pieces rather than let it fall. We recall the significance of the standard. It symbolised that cause, those values for which the combatants were fighting and prepared to die. So, her nuns not merely symbolised the heart of the Church, her nature, the reason for her existence, but, hidden away in their cloisters, actually lived out this central reality. If the standard falls, all is lost, the combatants lose heart and collapse in disarray. As Teresa points out, to carry the standard is no easy vocation.

> I find few true contemplatives who are not courageous and resolute in suffering; for if they are weak, the first thing the Lord does is to give them courage so that they may fear no trials that come to them.[14]

St Thomas Aquinas might claim – Friar Preacher that he was – that

> ... even as it is better to enlighten than merely to shine, so is it better to give to others the fruits of one's contemplation than merely to contemplate.[15]

But Teresa realised that to shine is to illumine, that the fruits of genuine contemplation are for others. Holiness, of its very nature reaches far beyond conscious experience, touching others at the roots of their being.

O my Jesus, how much a soul can do when ablaze with Thy love! What great value we ought to set on it and how we should beseech the Lord to allow it to remain in this life.[16]

The desire of her heart was to lead her daughters to such a love. This important insight of St Teresa, this explicit intention that the nuns of her Carmel, devoted exclusively to prayer with no external apostolate, should be in will and reality wholly apostolic, was absorbed into the understanding of the Church and given official recognition at the Second Vatican Council:

> Institutes which are entirely ordered towards contemplation in such a way that their members give themselves over to God alone in solitude and silence, in constant prayer and willing penance . . . have a hidden apostolic fruitfulness. No matter how pressing may be the needs of the active ministry, they must be left in their solitude.[17]

A clear statement, indeed.

We recall St John of the Cross's emphasis on the value to the Church and the world at large of the purely contemplative life, when lived to the full, allowing divine Love to take possession,

> . . . fulfilling the one thing necessary, to abide with God and to be continually occupied with His love. This He prizes and esteems to such a high degree that He reproved Martha because she wanted to withdraw Mary from His feet so as to occupy her in other activities in the Lord's service, considering that she was doing everything and Mary was resting with the Lord, the truth being just the contrary, for there is no better or more necessary work than love . . . for a very little of this pure love is more precious in the sight of God and the soul, and of greater value and profit to the Church, even though the soul appear to be doing nothing, than are all these other works together.[18]

Down the centuries, wherever the authentic charism of Carmel has prevailed, the torch has been handed on and with it the Order's motto of Elijah's cry, 'With zeal I have been zealous for the Lord God of Hosts.'

In more recent times, we have Elisabeth of Dijon offering herself: 'Spend all my substance for Your glory; let it distil, drop by drop for Your Church,' and Edith Stein, a convert from Judaism, relinquishing her outstanding professional and apostolic work, for the hidden life of Carmel, to offer herself for her martyred people: 'Human activity cannot help us but only the Passion of Christ.' These Carmelites have, in God's providence, found a public voice, but there have been and no doubt are, countless others who, like Mary of Bethany, pour out their lives over the feet of Christ, in what, to eyes other than the eyes of love, seems a meaningless gesture: 'To what purpose is this waste?' The censure is still heard and within the Church itself.

So great is the significance of St Thérèse of Lisieux that, deliberately, she has been left to the end. The immense importance of her life with its profound understanding of the Gospel, has been stressed over and over again by the highest authorities in the Church and finally, sealed by the title 'Doctor of the Church'. Her significance to Carmel cannot be overestimated and we shall have cause to refer to her again and again. Precisely in showing us the heart of the Gospel, isolating it, as it were, from falsifying accretions, she reinterprets the charism of Carmel, and reveals it simply as a most pure expression of the Gospel. She goes to its very heart and strips off the debris it has gathered in its passage down the centuries, and, often enough, redresses the balance. Her missionary spirit is so well known that there is no need to dwell on it. Even before she entered Carmel she was fired with desire to 'save souls for Jesus', to 'quench His thirst by giving Him souls'. This was her motive for entering Carmel. Her sister, Céline, tells us that Thérèse was not immune to the attraction of the missionary apostolate, even to finding it wise to resist reading the missionary magazines that came her way. It was her unwavering conviction that her work for souls lay within the silence and hiddenness of Carmel. This motive only gained in ardour as she grew in love for God. It must be so always. Today we are unlikely to conceive of 'souls falling, like autumn leaves, into hell', or even to speak of 'saving souls'. Thérèse grasped the ultimate truth of it all, the truth that enkindled her impassioned zeal, namely, that Love is not loved. She perceived that there were floods of infinite tenderness pent up in God's heart because human hearts will not receive them. And so she offered herself unconditionally, no matter what the consequences, to receive into her own small reality, their full force, and through her, she was convinced, they would inundate the world. 'In the heart of my mother the Church, I will be love.' This, it seems, has become for modern Carmelites, their interpretation of Elijah's, 'With zeal I have been zealous for the Lord God of hosts.'

Thérèse is the wonderful champion of ordinary people. We might think that Teresa herself, John of the Cross, Elisabeth of the Trinity and Edith Stein, are, after all, lofty souls, eagles and that Carmel is meant only for such. This is not so. The structure of the life – the horarium, the silence and aloneness, customs that lay stress on particular values, the 'detachment from created things' (unworldliness), obedience, the relationships between the sisters – all that makes the actual reality of Carmelite life, does indeed express great love for God, and a passionate

9

devotion. For most of those who embrace Teresa's Carmel, the expression far outstrips their actual state, at least to begin with, perhaps for many years afterwards, and sadly, maybe always. But Teresa believed, and experience proves, that a truly earnest, faithful observance does, in fact, provide an almost perfect situation for receiving a very great love of God. What must be stressed is that the structure must not be adapted to a lesser love. Teresa herself speaks firmly on the subject. She is discussing the harm done to a community by receiving unsuitable subjects and what she has in mind particularly is the person who wants to adapt the life to her own requirements, who thinks she knows best, who cannot accept to be taught, who has, basically, a worldly outlook. Of such a one she writes:

> Such a person will save her soul better elsewhere than here; she may even gradually reach a degree of perfection which she could not have attained here because we expected too much of her all at once. For although we allow time for the attainment of complete detachment and mortification in interior matters, in externals this has to be practised immediately, because of the harm which may befall the rest . . . [19]

She knew only too well how easy it is for the standard to fall. Of course we are shamed before the ideal, aware that we fall far short, but this must be accepted humbly and lived with and not evaded by a lowering of standard. No one has understood better than the Carmelite Thérèse, the true meaning of poverty of spirit and how this is the essence of Carmel. Yet we turn our backs on this when we seek a happier image of ourselves in an adapted life-style.

CHAPTER TWO

The Source

'This will always be the aim of our nuns – to be alone with
Him only.'[1] We cannot overestimate the importance of this
text for the understanding of the Carmelite charism. It
must be taken with the greatest seriousness. Clearly, St
Teresa is looking back to the sources of our Order, the
well-spring, the 'fountain of Elijah on Mount Carmel', to
'those early forefathers of ours from Mount Carmel'[2]
whose life was wholly eremitical; she is looking to the
Rule of St Albert, formulated and delivered to the 'hermits
living by the spring on Mount Carmel', between 1209 and
1214. This community of hermits had settled in an enclosure that nature itself had formed, now identified as the
Wadi-es-Siah. Throughout Western Europe in the
eleventh and twelfth centuries, eremiticism knew a
remarkable renaissance. Like the emergence of the mendi-
cant ideal of Dominic, Francis and others, eremiticism was
in great part a reaction to the decline in the monastic
ideal. Life in the great abbatial communities, with their
vast estates, wealth, and power, seemed in many instances,
a far cry from the simplicity of the Benedictine ideal of
seeking Christ.

Another important feature of this era was the passionate involvement with the Holy Land and our Saviour's

earthly life. Europe's manhood, prince and commoner alike, pledged themselves to win back and keep the Holy Land in Christian hands. Countless men and women, readily undertook the painful, perilous journey to Palestine, for the privilege of treading the ground that Jesus trod, visiting the places of his birth, his ministry and his death. Religious communities proliferated and this is the context, the spiritual environment, of the first Carmelites settled on Mount Carmel. Of their origins, we know nothing except that they were Western Europeans. They may have been crusaders; they may already have been living as hermits before coming together to form a community of 'brothers', but already we have a feature that is basic to the Carmelite ideal: the fruitful tension between eremiticism and community. Here is a community of hermits or, perhaps more correctly, here are hermits who have elected to form a community.

The Primitive Rule given to this community by Albert, the Latin Patriarch of Jerusalem, clearly defined the limits of life in common. The brothers were to choose a prior who was to safeguard the way of life, assign cells to the individual hermits, see to the needs of the community. To this prior the brothers promised obedience. The only common room was the oratory, built in the midst of the cells. Here, every morning, the community gathered for the celebration of Mass – a remarkable ordinance since at the time, daily attendance at Mass was not a normal practice for hermits – and here they assembled each Sunday for examination of their life together and for the correction of faults. Since the Rule prescribes total silence from after Vespers until after Terce the following morning, with a less strict silence at other times (though exhorting the brothers to be careful not to indulge in useless talk), we may presume that there was some intercourse between the brothers.

The greatest weight, as we would expect in a Rule for hermits, is laid on solitude. Each brother stayed night and day in the cell assigned to him, 'meditating on the law of the Lord and watching in prayer'. This prayer in solitude included whatever comprised the Canonical Hours. Each one took his meals alone and laboured to produce some handwork which could be bartered or sold for the support of the community.

With Saracen victories and loss of territory to the Christians, the community's situation became untenable. Alms from the flow of pilgrims ceased and the hermits were exposed to persecution. Emigration to Europe, begun in 1238, soon became total. In most cases this involved a radical change of climate, environment and culture and necessitated some adaptation of the Rule which had been designed for a particular group in a specific locality. The authorised changes of 1248 left the basic eremiticism untouched but ordained that the brethren should dine together and recite the Canonical Hours in common. Apart from necessary duties imposed by obedience, they were to remain alone in their separate cells with the same intent on constant prayer and attention to divine things. To bring the Order into conformity with the canonical pattern of religious life, the vows of poverty and chastity were added to that of obedience. The revised legislation removed the restriction of settlements to solitary places only; henceforth, they could be made in populated areas. It is easy to see that the sheer practicalities of life in Europe demanded these concessions, but easy also to see how the Order that came to birth in the solitude of the Wadi-es-Siah, was ill-fitted to withstand the pressures of the burgeoning urban life of medieval Europe, with its ferment of new learning and its newly created universities.

We need not concern ourselves over much with the chequered history of the Order, so far exclusively male, as it struggled to find a place and identity in medieval Europe. It lost the struggle to maintain eremiticism and took its place alongside the Mendicants. The second mitigation of the Rule of St Albert requested of Pope Eugenius IV and ceded by him in 1432, when the Order was at its lowest ebb, was but a legitimisation of the situation that actually prevailed, and the last stage of de-eremiticising, if one may so call it. As always, there were reactions and valiant attempts at reform, but our own concern is with the incorporation of women into the Order.

Various groups of *beatas* in different localities, were affiliated to the Order. *Beatas,* a distinctive category of devout women, need a word of explanation. What characterised them was their freedom. They belonged to no religious order, did not take public vows, were not 'burdened' with a weight of liturgical offices but cultivated a life of interiority and prayer, besides devoting themselves to good works. Often, they wore a distinctive dress, and some came together to form a community as happened with a group in Castile, which in 1479, formed the community of the Monastery of the Incarnation at Avila. Only in 1513 did it cease to be a *beaterio* and adopt a more regular life which included choral Office. It is not without significance, as will be revealed later, that this change occurred only twenty years or so before St Teresa took the habit.[3]

There has been a great deal of research into the social

14

structure prevailing in Spain in the fifteenth and sixteenth centuries and, more particularly, in Avila.[+] Many of these fascinating findings throw light on the Reform initiated by Teresa and reveal what a radical rejection it was of the worldly values permeating both civic and ecclesiastical life. Her fellow citizens, her relatives and acquaintances, the whole society in which she was born and in which she grew up, was obsessed with lineage, 'pure blood' (untainted, that is, by any Jewish or Moorish strain), reputation, honour, wealth and power. Civic and ecclesiastical life was wedded in this common passion and monastic institutions, too, entangled in a web of dynastic pride and prestige.

The foundress of the Monastery of the Incarnation, Dona Elvira Gonzalez de Medina, had been the concubine of a cathedral canon and archdeacon, Don Nuno Gonzalez del Aguila, and bore him four children. After his death she established a *beaterio* in her own house consisting of about fourteen women. Dona Elvira's group found favour with the king and queen of Spain who gave them land. The community knew a rapid expansion and within twenty years of its existence, counted over one hundred members; later, in Teresa's time, one hundred and fifty. Dona Elvira was following an established pattern whereby wealthy widows devoted their resources – their money, and their estates – to founding monastic institutions which then they ruled as abbesses, maintaining absolute control. Dona Elvira could choose her successor and, in fact, appointed one of her daughters, thus ensuring the 'dynasty'. (Later reforms introduced electoral rights for the community.) Realistically, we must recognise the passion for prestige and influence in these monastic institutions, which were part of the fabric of society. We have only to read of the virulent opposition on the part of the civic authorities, all members of the privileged aristocracy, to the foundation of the seemingly unobtrusive, poor convent of St Joseph, to realise that vested interests were at stake; this new concept of monastic life, owing nothing to patronage, offering nothing tangible even by way of obligatory suffrages for the dead, threatened their most prized values.

It is hardly likely that a foundation such as that of the Incarnation, lacking roots, lacking real spiritual charism, would be a fitting setting for a deeply committed spiritual life, nor likely to breed in its members an understanding of the Rule of Carmel which, theoretically, they embraced. But God can be loved anywhere, in any circumstances and Teresa assures us of the genuine holiness of some of her companions; not a few followed her into the Reform. What is clear from her own story is that, within the monastery itself, the same worldly values prevailed and she herself was caught up in them. Candidly she admits that she deliberately chose the Incarnation, over against the edifying, strict community to which her father had entrusted her when she was living dangerously, because it housed friends and relatives and was easygoing. After her conversion, when her eyes were finally opened to the utter vanity of it all, she could write:

> I did not know how I was going to live: you could have seen that my poor soul was worn out. It hears itself being told always to occupy its thoughts with God and to be sure to keep them fixed on Him so that it may escape from all kinds of dangers. On the other hand, it discovers that it must not fail to observe a single point of etiquette, less it give offence to those who think this etiquette essential to their honour. I used to be simply worn out by all this: my attempts to satisfy people were never-ending, for, to study to

please them as I would, I was always making mistakes, and, as I say, these are never overlooked as being unimportant. And is it the case that in religious Orders excuses are made for such things? It might be thought reasonable that we should be excused from these observances. But no; they say that convents should be courts and schools of good breeding.[5]

Later, when she had been asked to spend some years in her old monastery in order to effect a reform, Teresa would write: 'Oh . . . to have experienced the tranquillity of our (Discalced) houses, and then to find oneself in this hurly burly! I don't know how anyone can live here at all . . . ', and tells her correspondent that she is cutting down the nuns' diversions and limiting their freedom.[6]

All the same, Teresa loved her convent and was fond of her 'cell' (a little suite of rooms in fact, where she could entertain her friends!). She was caught up in the same pastimes as others – though not without torments of conscience as, gradually, through dogged perseverance in prayer, she began to see more and more how counter to the truth and values of Jesus were the 'vanities' that absorbed her. On her own admission, she had neither the spiritual enlightenment nor strength to resist the pressures of worldliness and gives a poignant account of her long and painful struggle, 'falling and rising', to be faithful to her obligations as a religious and to the practice of prayer. Our Lord, she tells us, came to her rescue, with graces of prayer culminating in a thoroughgoing conversion and passionate commitment to Christ. She became dissatisfied with life at the Incarnation and longed for greater seclusion.

As well as frequent perusal of the Constitutions of the Order,[7] which, of course, were based on and included the

Rule of St Albert as mitigated in 1432, Teresa would be familiar with stories of the hermits of Mount Carmel,

> those holy fore-fathers of ours: the sufferings they bore – solitude, cold, hunger, burning heat – with no one to complain to but God, and they were not made of iron but of flesh and blood like ourselves,[8]

and with the legendary material (assumed most likely to be authentic facts) surrounding them:

> . . . after the example of that holy man and solitary the prophet Elijah, they led the hermit life on Mount Carmel, and especially on that part which is above the city of Porphyr, today called Haifa, near the spring called Elijah's Spring, not far from the monastery of the blessed virgin Margaret, in little cells like so many hives where, as bees of the Lord, they produced the honey of spiritual sweetness.[9]

Fully alive to Love's demands, Teresa must have looked with desire towards that pure spring of the Order's beginning, contrasting starkly as it did with the turgid waters in which she found herself. The meeting with Marie of Jesus, a *beata* who shared her desire to found a reformed convent of the Order, was the occasion of Teresa's introduction to the Rule as it was before the mitigation of 1432.[10] It is this version that she consistently refers to as the Primitive Rule, which, as we have seen, it was not. It represented all she longed for and needed: a deep solitude, silence, simplicity and purity of life, freedom from the crippling bondage of worldliness that had held her back from God. Eremitical in the truest sense – she herself was to reveal its meaning in a most creative way – it was an expression of fervent dedication.

'Understanding for the first time the nature of the Rule and realising that its way was of greater perfection,'[11] she was the more strongly motivated and determined to found a community where it would be lived in its first purity.

The *beata* Marie pointed out the radical poverty the Rule enjoined, forbidding not only personal possessions but also communal possession of revenues: the hermits were to be maintained by alms and the work of their hands. This ordinance, hitherto not foreseen or intended by Teresa, won her heart. She determined that her house, and subsequent houses, should be founded in poverty, without revenues, dependent on alms and what the nuns could earn by their work. Not many years later,[12] she was faced with a choice of priorities as to which took first place in the charism of Carmel: total prayer, or adherence to the pattern of radical poverty. She was certain that prayer was the heart of the charism and other treasured values had to be sacrificed to it.

Teresa's choice has important consequences for us. We shall see throughout that there was no romantic, literal interpretation of the Rule. With wonderful freedom she adapted it to the very different circumstances of sixteenth century Spain and its women. Teresa's desire for the pure simplicity of life of the early hermits never made her unrealistic. For instance, it is likely that the majority of these hermits were illiterate for only those 'who know their letters'[13] are bound to the recitation of the Hours; and, following the emigration to Europe, we have the French Prior General berating the pretensions of 'illiterates' aspiring to be preachers and 'doctors of spiritual wounds and diseases in the confessional . . . ignorant of learning and law . . . '. By this time they had the opportunity to be otherwise.[14] St Teresa would guard against this mental impoverishment. Her daughters must be able to read and the illiterate taught. Whereas, the refectory reading of scripture apart, the Rule makes no mention of it, Teresa's constitutions speak explicitly of the necessity of reading and assign to it an hour a day.

The years Teresa spent in the Incarnation were not wasted; on the contrary, they afforded her great experience. She learned at first hand of the things that made total dedication to God extremely difficult, if not impossible, for the majority of nuns in spite of their good will. Chief among these obstacles was the lack of enclosure which allowed the nuns freedom to stay outside the monastery in the houses of relatives and friends. The very size of the community made discipline impossible and this was a further obstacle to steady devotion. Furthermore, it over-taxed the community's financial resources. As material goods were not held in common, the well-to-do (of whom Teresa was one) could live comfortably, but the poor were almost destitute. It is hardly to be wondered at, that the nuns seized the opportunity to accept the hospitality of seculars and cultivate patronage by charm and flirtatious behaviour in the convent parlours. Teresa saw clearly that if a community was to live a life devoted to prayer it must be free from financial worries and reasonably confident of not lacking necessities. True to her first ideal – that her nuns were to rely on alms and the sale of their work – she took good care to found her houses in populated, wealthy districts, and to limit the number of nuns to thirteen or fourteen.

It was during her years at the Incarnation that Teresa learned the value of spiritual friendship: 'I needed the help of others, who would take me by the hand and raise me up.'[15] And: 'After God, I owe it to such friends that I am not in hell.[16] She also wrote:

> I wish we five, who now love each other in Christ, could make an
> agreement together . . . [that] we might contrive to meet some-
> times to undeceive each other and to advise one another as to ways
> in which we might amend our lives and be more pleasing to God;
> for there is no one who knows himself as well as he is known by
> those who see him if they observe him lovingly and are anxious to
> help him.[17]

If Teresa experienced the harm of disordered relationships and of undisciplined community living, she was
convinced that real friendship and a well-ordered community had an inestimable part to play in spiritual growth: '
. . . the great means of progress for a soul is converse with
God's friends'.[18] She was influenced by, and herself became
part of, a great movement of reform sweeping through
Spain. While the Council of Trent hammered out dogmas
and examined means to reform systems, men and women
of spirituality were working at the grass roots to reform
the clergy, instruct and inspire the laity and catechise children. Many of Teresa's friends were part of this
movement.

To conclude: Teresa brought all her spiritual graces,
her passionate love for Christ and the wisdom it engen-
dered, together with the rich human experience of the
twenty years or so of life spent in a monastery of the mitigation, to create an environment, a way of life wholly true
to the Rule of St Albert, that would give to women of her
day ideal conditions for directing themselves to God in
striving to follow Jesus perfectly. The spirit of Carmel is
wholly Christocentric and incarnational. St Teresa repu-
diated every spirituality that bypassed the Sacred
Humanity. As a young nun, anxiously seeking a way of

prayer but lacking guidance, she was lured away for a time, from contemplation of Jesus and found it hard, later on, to forgive herself for this mistake. In the fullness of spiritual maturity, she authoritatively reaffirms the centrality of the Sacred Humanity in the way of transforming prayer.[19] The Rule is evidence that the Order from its origins was Christocentric. As already remarked, the crusades, the pilgrimages, the religious communities of Palestine, including the hermits of Mount Carmel, were inspired by an enormous interest in Jesus' earthly life. The Old Testament reference in the Rule to the 'the law of the Lord' as the subject of meditation, would surely refer to the mysteries of Jesus. The 'law' used in this sense, even in the Old Testament, covered the whole of God's loving dealings with human beings, what we would call salvation history, of which the incarnation, life, passion, death and resurrection of Jesus are the alpha and omega.

Teresa's own humanity, her recognition of human needs, her earthliness and practical common sense keep the way of Carmel firmly earthed and incarnational. Christocentricism made her profoundly ecclesial, Catholic to her core, though far from blind to the glaring sinfulness of the Church. She knew the meaning and saw the immense value of the sacraments, appreciated even sacramentals, and grasped and made her own the 'communion of saints'. As we would expect of one devoted to Jesus, his mother held a special place in Teresa's love and, unusually, Jesus' foster-father, Joseph. Devotion to Our Lady, is, of course, traditional in the Order. It was claimed that the first oratory of the hermits was dedicated to her and, very early in the Order's history, the brothers were called the Brothers of the Blessed Virgin. From the very beginning, the presence of Our Lady, whether adverted to or not, pervades our monasteries, the Virgin of Nazareth, whose humility and surrender drew the Almighty down to be one with our lowliness.

CHAPTER THREE

The Return to Source

Enclosure

Teresa takes her little community back to 'the desert', that is, the Order's source – a solitary place, more solitary, more protected perhaps than the Wadi-es-Siah, but in the heart of a city.

She does this by providing a strict material enclosure which will free the community to fulfil the purpose of the Order: '. . . prayer and contemplation – because that was the first principle of our Order'[1]; ' . . . to abide with God and to be continually occupied with His love'[2]; 'our Primitive Rule tells us to pray without ceasing'.[3]

We must recognise here a free, clear-eyed choice on Teresa's part. Her option preceded the Council of Trent's imposition of enclosure on all women religious. She did not, as some would claim, seek refuge in enclosure from the zealous scrutiny of the Inquisition. Someone feeling the need to keep her head down is hardly likely to have used her pen so freely. In a period of more than ordinary misogyny and repression of anything remotely bordering on 'illuminism', Teresa had indeed to be wary. Illuminism is the name given to a particular movement in sixteenth-century Spain which claimed that personal, spiritual experience had an authority that superseded that of the teaching Church. The *illuminati* saw no need for the sacraments or any form of priestly 'mediation'. The sect abounded in visions and other 'mystical' phenomena. Against her wishes, for she foresaw the peril, Teresa's own visionary experiences became public. Although she aroused the suspicion of some members of the Inquisition, her devotion to the sacraments, the cult of the saints, love of images and of other genuinely Catholic devotions, set her apart from the *illuminati.*⁺ Besides which, Teresa had a lifelong psychological need of male support and approval which served to conceal her spiritual authority behind a screen of submission: we have only to see how cleverly, how skilfully she manipulates in the *The Way of Perfection*. The authorities have proscribed books of devotion. Even the scriptures must be carefully censored so as not to lead foolish women astray. These same empty-headed creatures must be kept to vocal prayer only, reciting their *Paters* and *Aves*, and get on with their spinning. Teresa will dutifully observe this injunction – no one could fault her – and sets herself to teach her daughters how to pray the Our Father well. To her astonishment(!) she discovers that, in so doing, she has been telling them all about mystical contemplation.

Teresa had to hand the venerated holy woman, Mari Diaz, a model she could well have imitated and whom she greatly admired. This ascetic and mystic spent herself for the same ends on which Teresa had set her heart: the purification and sanctification of the Church, the reform of the clergy, fostering and teaching a spirituality of the heart, catechising children, helping the poor, counselling men and women of all classes, working alongside the great reforming figures, the preachers and theologians defending the Church. Mari Diaz exercised an enormous influence for good in the city of Avila as in other places. The newly-formed Company of Jesus (Jesuits) owed much to her and learned members of the Order sought her spiritual advice. She was vital to the creation of the Tridentine seminary in Avila which was one of the first in Spain. Although eventually domiciled in a little place attached to a church, there was no question of an enclosure in Teresa's sense. She survived unscathed by the Inquisition until her death in 1572.[5]

Not without reason could it be said that Teresa was ideally suited for the life of a *beata* after the fashion of Mari Diaz and, humanly speaking, there was nothing to stop her from adopting it. Teresa's own community of the Incarnation seems to have retained, very understandably, the mentality and characteristics of the *beaterio* it once had been. During her early, formative years as a religious, some of the older nuns, and possibly those responsible for her initiation, were former *beatas*. It would not be easy to acquire a wholly different outlook, let alone transmit it. The habit of living outside the monastery, often of a large proportion of the community at one time, is an indication of the prevalence of this mentality. How could the obligation to Choral Office be taken seriously in such a situation?

Teresa was well aware that she had an enormous influence for good wherever she went and that her presence in the house of seculars aroused people to a love of God and desire for prayer. From her youth upwards Teresa had proof of it. For herself, freedom from enclosure gave her opportunities otherwise unavailable. She found directors that understood her: it was while staying in a friend's house that she met St Peter of Alcantara whose support and guidance she sorely needed; and in the same house likewise, Maria of Jesus. She encountered influential people who became her friends and helped her with her foundations, and some of the young women whom she met joined her Reform, notably Maria of St Joseph, one of her most gifted, trusted and best loved daughters.

Far from developing this more free form of monastic life – and, at the time she first decided on her course of action, one that was still legitimate for enclosure had not yet been enforced – Teresa made an unwavering choice of a life strictly enclosed and 'unfree'.

This is the more impressive in that, by now, she knew that she herself no longer needed enclosure as she had done in her early years and the loss of which she bewailed: 'It was a very bad thing for me not to be in a convent that was enclosed.'[6]

Now her absorption in God was her enclosure and, as she says, nothing and no one could distract her; what had previously been harmful was a positive help, everything a means by which she could love God.[7] Even so, Teresa became unshakeably convinced that God wanted her to found a house in the strictest enclosure and it was to be a return to the eremitical origins of the Order. So, what seemed the obvious spiritual way for her, was transcended. As far as she was concerned, she would disappear from the human scene and her great gifts lie unused. What a waste! Yet Teresa knew, as those who were to follow her would know, that nothing would be wasted. They would be committing the whole expanse of their being to the creative action of Divine Love; exposing themselves, undefended, to the God whose very nature is to give. To do this in the way in which they felt themselves called, demanded a strict enclosure. Teresa writes to her brother, Don

Lorenzo de Cepeda, for financial help with her proposed foundation:

> They [the nuns] will live in the strictest enclosure, never going out, and seeing no one without veils over their faces, and the foundation of their lives will be prayer and mortification.[8]

Her legislation, her injunctions to the Visitator to watch over its observance with scrupulous care, all testify to her deep concern that her hermit community should dwell in complete seclusion. We see from Teresa's own account – and more graphically from that of her biographer, Julian of Avila, who accompanied her and her party of nuns to the place of projected foundations – to what lengths she carried her desire that her nuns remain secluded. When putting up at an inn, she would improvise an enclosure by means of a curtain, appointing one sister to deal with whoever wished to contact the group. The nuns travelled with their veils lowered or in closed carriages, and this in the broiling heat. 'Surely,' we might think, 'this is going too far! What harm would it do the nuns to dispense with such precautions when on a journey?' Obviously, Teresa did not think it was going too far. She was not playing a romantic game.

Teresa is making a clear statement both to the 'world' but also, and more importantly, to her nuns. What is it she is saying? That they have turned their backs, once for all, absolutely, on the false values of their culture

> ... the vanity and parade of the world, in which, according to its own standards, they might have been happy.[9]

Looking more closely at this culture – insofar as we know it – we can readily perceive that what underlies it is the basic drive of the human heart for satisfaction, affirmation, a sense of value, of importance, a desire to be loved, admired, a fear of unimportance and powerlessness, of being unable to control one's life and therefore of slipping into oblivion. Christian faith roots us, grounds us in God. It reveals our true identity and meaning which lies only in God, the God of Jesus. Faith 'dies' to the 'world', to the passionate search for meaning within the limits of the world. To choose to dwell in 'the desert' is a decision to cast oneself totally on God; to look for affirmation, love, fulfilment only from God. There can hardly be a more radical choice. Drastic surgery, if you like! Teresa, ever realistic, knows that no matter how sincere, how radical the choice, how desirous a person is to live for God alone, a long purification involving a most generous effort on her part and the profound action of God is needed before the desire is reality:

> It is a hard thing to withdraw from ourselves and oppose ourselves, because we are very close to ourselves and love ourselves dearly.[10]

Teresa leaves no stone unturned to provide the very best conditions for the detachment from self that leaves Divine Love free to bestow Itself. Precautions concerning all aspect of enclosure which, to us, may seem excessive, had this in view. Our own expressions of enclosure may differ: the supervision she ordained would be abhorrent to us. What is unchanging and basic to the Teresian Carmel is strict enclosure, a true desert where we choose to remain and for the same purpose for which she created it. It is incumbent on us to keep a most careful watch and to think out carefully every point involved. A weakening of enclosure inevitably means a loss of the true spirit, of the very purpose of Carmel.

> My soul is occupied,
> And all my substance in His service;
> Now I guard no flock,
> Nor have I any other employment:
> My sole occupation is love.

> If then, on the common land
> I am no longer seen and found,
> You will say that I am lost;
> That, being enamoured,
> I lost myself; and yet was found.[11]

Although Teresa speaks glowingly of the vocation to the desert, she fully realises that it is God's will only for the few. She is far from wanting the 'preachers and theologians' to remove themselves from the battlefield and betake themselves to an enclosed monastery. She positively dissuades them when they express the desire.[12] What she wants for them is to grow in true spirituality and, as already remarked, she sees the vocation of her nuns to be vital to this.

To be called to live a life of total prayer in a strict enclosure is a vocation, a particular charism in the Church and in the world. It is a ministry to the Church and to the world.

> Now there are varieties of gifts, but the same Spirit; and there are varieties of service, but the same Lord; and there are varieties of working, but it is the same God who inspires them all in everyone. To each is given the manifestation of the Spirit for the common good.[13]

No one can claim that his\her vocation is better or higher

than another. The important thing is that each of us should live to the utmost the vocation assigned to us. We cannot be holy outside our own vocation, for the Spirit is fully available to us only within that vocation. It holds within it everything we need to surrender us to God and make us fruitful in the Church. The vocation to Carmel is very demanding but since God has given it to us it will 'fit' us and, provided that we are faithful to its demands, we will grow humanly and spiritually. There are many ways of evading these far-reaching, deeply penetrating demands.

The desert of Carmel where the first hermits dwelt was no sandy waste. On the contrary, it was renowned for its beauty. And rightly, we can speak of our enclosure as 'a garden enclosed'. St John of the Cross encircles his drawing of the Ascent of the Mount with the lovely words: 'I have brought you into the land of Carmel that you may eat the fruits and the good things thereof.' However, this can be only for those who embrace the cross, who set their hearts as steadfastly as they can on loving God only. 'To live alone with God alone.' There is an aspect of desert living that must be faced and embraced if we are to understand and live the vocation profoundly and therefore grasp the purpose of a strict enclosure. 'Desert' usually calls up a bleak, exposed terrain; a land of no shelter, and yes, our vocation is to live all the time, defencelessly exposed to God's self-bestowing love, God, a consuming fire. This may sound dramatic if not romantic but what is entailed is a progressive spiritual impoverishment. Our great authorities, St Teresa and St John of the Cross, each in their own way, insist on the radical nature of the asceticism required if a human person is to be wholly surrendered to love, made one with Love. Detachment – this will be a watchword for both of them; detachment that is, ultimately, from our self-centred self. Though 'a soul that is perfect can be detached and humble anywhere'[14] it is our vocation to attain this detachment in the desert:

> ... the whole manner of life we are trying to live is making us, not only nuns but hermits and leading us to detachment from all created things.[15]

No one can pretend that it is easy. In the desert, the human heart is deprived of many, many things which would protect it from the fierce rays of the sun or the biting winds. Exposed to God, sooner or later, its experience will be of spiritual indigence, helplessness and sinfulness. In the 'world' one can be bolstered up by the affirmation of friends, a career, diverse interests, intense activity, to name a few of the things whereby we tend to hide from ourselves and acquire a *persona* with which we face the world. The desert strips us of all these pseudo faces; we might find the undoing bearable if it were accompanied by an inner assurance that we are getting somewhere, coming close to God, but this is unlikely.

> Only humility is of any use here, and this is not acquired by the understanding but by a clear perception of the truth, which comprehends in one moment what could not be attained over a long period by the labour of the understanding – namely, that we are nothing and that God is infinitely great.[16]

Such 'riches' as these, the gold of pure wisdom, are found in the desert by those who will stay there defenceless.

Our intention in this chapter is merely to establish the fact that a strict enclosure belongs to the very essence of Carmel, an expression of its profound eremiticism. It may well be that of no other contemplative orders of nuns can this be said. In choosing it, Teresa was not conforming, not a victim of her conditioning. For her an appreciation of enclosure belongs to the vocation and is one of the signs of genuineness.[17] We must be realistic. This appreciation need not be emotional and for everyone at times enclosure will be experienced as a sacrifice. It is rightly called an asceticism. However, living within it, surrendering herself to the life-style, a woman with a true vocation soon realises that she needs it as a fish needs its pool. The fact that she finds some enjoyment when for an unavoidable reason she must go outside, is a perfectly healthy reaction, but she will not be comfortable for long and will want to get back to the monastery as soon as she can. This strict enclosure is not imposed on unwilling people, only another instance of female oppression, but is something freely chosen and desired because, for those called to Carmel, it is experienced as necessary for their complete surrender to God.

Romantic notions must not blind us to the fact that living in the desert has its dangers. Enclosure cuts off many of the normal means for human development. Believing as we do that God does indeed call some 'daughters of the Church' into the desert we must be quite sure that it is never for psychic diminishment. God is pledged to bring them to human fulfilment without these normal means and therefore their commitment is in itself, an act of trust.

That being said, nevertheless, it is our bounden duty to ensure that our enclosure contains fundamental requirements. God asks the sacrifice of certain great human means: sexual expression in the context of love, forging a career and so on. The desert, of itself, cuts down radically on enjoyments, interests, opportunities . . . all of which are, or are meant to be, created means to God. We give God what God asks but do not try to give what is not asked. God positively wants our human development and our limited space must enclose a high quality of life. (This will be developed later.) Teresa's Constitutions fasten such a tight cordon around enclosure by way of material barriers and intensive supervision as to make infringement virtually impossible. Today, such material barriers as double iron grilles and 'turns', and constant invigilation are undesirable and counterproductive. Now the onus is on the individual sister. Each one is responsible for her fidelity to the letter and spirit of enclosure. This will be discussed when we consider the eremitical aspects within the enclosure itself.

CHAPTER FOUR

Life of Dedicated Love

> I determined to do the little that was in me – namely, to follow
> the evangelical counsels as perfectly as I could, and to see that
> the few nuns who are here should do the same, confiding in the
> great goodness of God who never fails to help those who for-
> sake all things for His sake.[1]

The evangelical counsels

In common with all forms of religious life, Carmel is
grounded on the three evangelical counsels of obedience,
poverty and chastity. To claim this is to claim that Carmel
is grounded on Jesus, for to pledge oneself to live by these
counsels is a particular – and we may say, radical – way of
following him, of being his disciple. Rightly does St
Teresa equate it with forsaking all things for his sake.

To do justice to these three counsels, to reveal their
depth and draw out all their implications, is matter for a
whole book. Here we must confine ourselves to a brief
survey. It was Teresa's expressed intention to create a way
of life which was as perfect a following of the counsels as
she could devise and if we do all we can to understand the
prescriptions and demands of the Rule and Constitutions,
and with God's grace live them faithfully, we will be following the evangelical counsels as perfectly as possible.

Why has the Church, from a very early time, not merely sanctioned but positively encouraged men and women who feel themselves so called, to make the great renunciations involved in the counsels? How do they justify the appellation 'evangelical'? Why are they called 'counsels of perfection'? It is right that we ask these questions for the answers are not obvious. The better we understand the more likely we are to live our vows intelligently and fruitfully. There is always a danger of leaving vital things unexamined, of imbibing assumptions that are not wholly in accord with the truth and then transmitting them to others. This is especially true in the case of our vows of obedience and chastity.

The vows affect three great human powers or rights, those that belong to our nature and, as such, are God-given: the power of choosing or free will; the right to possess a fair proportion of created goods; the right to exercise our sexual powers, marry and beget children. These powers or rights cover the whole way of being human creatures in this world. It is God's will that by their proper exercise, men and women develop themselves and one another and come to fulfilment. And yet we claim that some are called by God to renounce these God-given rights which, from our ordinary standpoint, are necessary for human fulfilment. It is further claimed that this radical renunciation of such great human goods finds its justification in Jesus. How?

To believe in Jesus, to base one's life on Jesus and the God Jesus reveals, is to recognise and to stake everything on a fulfilment that lies in God alone, not finite, not 'of this world'. Such is God's great plan of love, that for which God gave all he has, 'even His own Son'; that for which Jesus laid down his earthly life. Every Christian to be worthy of the name, must enter into this plan: that is to say that his\her movement towards legitimate human ful- filment must be plunged into the 'Paschal Mystery', into Jesus' dying to this world, to all its limitation and sinful- ness, in order to enter into the limitless life of God. The normal path to God is through the full exercise of these three human powers. Only faith can tell us of this other way, and a way that is as necessary as is the normal one, if the whole human family is to become what God wants it to be. We, along with many other men and women throughout the ages, are aware that we are called to this other way, the way of renunciation. Our awareness takes the form of need, a realisation – very personal and indi- vidual – that if we are to love God fully, then these renunciations are necessary. This sacrifice is legitimate only when informed by faith and sustained by trust in God, by a persistent reliance on Divine Love, sure that this Love, which wills absolutely our total humanness, will bring us to fulfilment through these renunciations. A life-long commitment to all that they entail, is a powerful, compelling witness to the God of Jesus as the absolute and only fulfilment of every human heart, a fulfilment that, of necessity, surpasses all that we could conceive, let alone achieve. Unless arising from and expressing such faith and trust, the vows are meaningless and harmful.

We know that St Teresa considered obedience vital to union with God ' . . . there is no path which leads more quickly to the highest perfection'.[2] Belonging as we do to another era and to a culture and social order very different from that of sixteenth-century Spain, our practical expres- sions of obedience will differ in some respects from Teresa's own and those she taught her contemporaries, but obedience itself must be every bit as radical. A matriarchal, autocratic exercise of authority such as pertained in her time and for centuries afterwards, is no longer valid and this affects the response obedience will take. The meaning, the intent is the same: a handing over of self, a surrender of the right to control our own life even down to daily details.

The revised formula for religious profession no longer makes explicit that the vow of obedience is made, under God, to the prioress of the community. The old formula read:

> I, Sister N., make my solemn profession and I promise obedience, poverty and chastity to God, to the Most Blessed Virgin Mary of Mount Carmel, and to you, Reverend Mother Prioress, and to your successors.

Now, the vows are made only to God, in the presence of the prioress and with the community to witness. However, both formulas make clear that we vow obedience, poverty and chastity according to the Rule and Constitutions of the Order, and these express unambiguously the obligation of obedience to the head of the community. The advantage of the new formula is that it vividly expresses the meaning of religious obedience as the dedication of self to the welfare of the community and of the whole Church. Obedience is shown as the gift of self to others, true servanthood. We no longer belong to ourselves, we are for others, wholly at their service. Obedience to the prioress is implicit in that it belongs to her to ensure that the vocation is faithfully lived; that each sister and the community as a whole, have everything that is needed for this purpose. This entails organisation, assignment of duties and many similar things. As the legislator, Albert of Jerusalem, ordained, regarding the prior: 'Everything

shall be done according to his will and direction . . .'.[3] So
the authority of the prioress is entirely at the service of,
and circumscribed by, the dedication that she herself and
all the sisters have made to belong wholly to God, 'for
Christ's body, the Church' in the way of Carmel. (The
office of prioress and the sisters' relations with her will
have a separate chapter.)

By our solemn vow of poverty we renounce absolutely
our right to possess. There is nothing whatever we may
consider our own. We are testifying that we believe that
no created thing can satisfy the human heart; that we do
not need the self-affirmation material goods seem to provide. According to means, the clothes we wear, the place
where we live, the furnishings of our home – house, flat,
bedsitter – maybe our career, are perfectly legitimate ways
of expressing our individuality, who we think we are, the
kind of person we would like to be and present to others.
By our vow of poverty we disclaim the need for the self-
affirmation that money can give, certain that each of us
has her absolute value in the eternal mind and heart of
God, that God alone knows our true identity and is totally
committed to bringing us to its full realisation. Again, by
money, we can to some extent control our circumstances
and defend our interests. Vowing poverty, we choose to
live out in a radical way the truth that we are utterly
dependent on God, and look to God to provide all we need
through our community. Teresa gives us many directives
in regard to poverty for she saw its great spiritual potential.

Our vow of chastity affirms most powerfully, searchingly and often painfully, that God unseen, unfelt, is
nevertheless all-sufficing Beauty, Goodness and Love and
has absolute claim over our hearts and bodies. More will

be said of this vow when we discuss community relation-ships and friendship. Here it suffices to make the important point, misunderstood or at least overlooked in the past, that what we renounce in this vow are the sexual acts which signify the total gift of self to another and normally lead to and are consummated in marriage. We do not renounce our sexuality and our capacity for human love and friendships. We consciously take God, take Jesus Our Lord, as the supreme Love of our hearts. We are, by faith, certain that in him we have in inconceivable totality, the perfect knowledge and understanding, the utterly tender and faithful devotion that we naturally long for from a human person. We try in our turn to give our-selves unreservedly until death.

CHAPTER FIVE

The Charism Embodied

The structure of life – the horarium

St Teresa passed five happy years with her companions in the newly-founded monastery of St Joseph. From the moment of its inception in her mind to its actual foundation, she had had time to think out its daily routine. These five years were ones of practical experimentation and, no doubt, the little group would have modified the pattern of the day until a truly satisfactory rhythm was found. By 1567, Teresa had framed Constitutions which stabilised a manner of life wholly in conformity with the Rule of St Albert, which she and her companions found

> . . . works most smoothly . . . [is] easy to endure and pleasant to carry out, and there is every facility for it being kept permanently by those who rejoice in Christ their Spouse in solitude.

She continues:

> If anyone thinks the Rule a harsh one, let her blame her own lack of spirituality and not our observance; for it can be borne quite easily by people who are not in the least robust, but really delicate, if they have sufficient spirituality'.[1]

Our lives are made up of days and our days of hours. Time moves on inexorably. Eternal life, that is, God's own life shared with us, flows here and now within time to be received or rejected. Time is given to us in order that eternal life may grow to fullness within us. Time is precious and demands that we hoard it like misers. Each moment – literally each moment – contains its own offer of Divine Love, a choice to love God or merely satisfy our own desires. As Teresian Carmelites we are given a means that guards against the squandering of time and enables us to use it to the full, devoting it entirely to loving God; namely, a strict, fixed horarium. In Teresa's mind this embodies the spirit, the devotion, the gift of self which are the whole purpose of her Reform. Her first Constitutions begin: 'Matins are to be said after nine o'clock . . . ' Matins is the first Hour of the liturgical day, and she takes us through the liturgical day until its completion in Compline on the following evening, pausing to say something on the various components that mark the day: the liturgy of the Hours, Mass and Communion, reading, work, silence, etc. The choice to build her Constitutions around the daily horarium is significant. After all, it is daily life that is life! Principles, ideals are not life unless embodied in day to day living. We might take delight in expatiating on the meaning, the beauty, the charism of the Order, but the question uppermost in an aspirant's mind and that she is eager to ask is: 'How do you spend the day?'

In 1581, at the first General Chapter of the newly established province of the Discalced Carmelite Friars, Teresa's Constitutions were redesigned and shaped into canonical form. She herself and all the nuns were consulted before the final drafting of the Alcala text. In substance it is wholly in accord with Teresa's original, allowing for a few modifications, some of which she asked for and a few she merely tolerated. The revised and, for then, definitive version of the Constitutions follows the order of the Rule of St Albert, not structured on the daily horarium as is St Teresa's own text. No doubt this re-fashioning was essential from the canonical point of view but the dynamic, forthright character of the original was lost.

There is nothing leisurely about the Teresian daily schedule. It is detailed, every hour accounted for with little room for self-pleasing. It expresses – and demands – a constant gift of self. To live this strict routine, to choose with all one's heart to be fastened to it, is indeed to lay down one's life and herein lies our constant 'Yes', our obedience. There are those today who claim that such a highly regulated life belongs to another age when women were less developed and mature. Mature people, it is said, should be allowed greater freedom of choice, trusted to do all they ought without this 'regimentation', without these relentless bells! This is to underestimate the radicality of the gift of self our vocation demands:

> Let them never say: 'This does not matter. We are being too particular about this.' O my daughters, everything matters if it is not helping us to make progress.[2]

It is to underestimate too our innate egotism and blindness. We need this firm, fixed daily structure if we are to give ourselves wholly to God, to fulfil our vocation in the Church. It ensures – provided we embrace it with a generous heart – that we remain all day long exposed to God's purifying and transforming love. It protects us from the tyranny of our moods, our times of blindness and spiritual weakness, from our whims and the vagaries of self-will. Properly understood, it is a gift, a grace, our best friend – provided that we really do want to love God with our whole heart, mind and body; if we want to live for others and not for ourselves. Self-deception is easy and, in making our daily life more flexible, more in accord with our own ideas of what a contemplative existence should be like; we can, in fact, be shirking the self-detachment that a very great love of God demands. A genuine contemplative life means a selfless life, a life handed over to God, under the constant purifying and transforming action of the Holy Spirit. It has nothing to do with an emotional state, with the feeling of peace and tranquillity that maybe allows for a sense of the divine presence. The peace that Jesus offers, his own peace, is not rooted in the emotions and maybe is not experienced on the conscious level. Jesus' peace is the utter security he has in the Father's love and in his own surrender to the Father. Therefore, to live a genuine contemplative life does not mean avoiding all physical and emotional stress so that we can pass our days in unruffled tranquillity. It means trustfully and lovingly submitting to the purifying action of the Holy Spirit in the demands of the Rule and of life in common, so as to be rid of our absorbing selfishness. Of course there is a kind of stress that we must try to avoid, caused, for instance, by poor organisation, or overwork. Teresa herself was anxious that the sisters should not work under stress and in her Constitutions forbids the assignments of tasks that must be completed within a set time limit. Good organisation, silence, the practice of virtue, a thoughtful, sensitive charity, and mutual trust among the sisters, go far in creating a truly easeful, relaxed atmosphere. All this belongs to a faithful living of the Rule. Nevertheless, it is impossible to eliminate all stress and certainly we may not try to do so by changing the character of the life-style.

When, as individuals, we experience stress, before taking steps to change our circumstances, we need to be honest with ourselves and maybe recognise that our stress is a signal (and therefore to be welcomed) that we are seeking something other than God: wanting, maybe, the approval and admiration of others, desperate to please, to appear good, afraid to fail in some way. The answer, of course, lies not in mitigating the observance but in exposing ourselves on the cross of the Rule to the healing, purifying love of God. In this way we are freed from the self-preoccupation which is the root of our stress. As was pointed out earlier, Teresa's Carmel is an expression of and a means to a passionate love of God. The strict horarium is essential to the charism.

A notable characteristic of the horarium is the alternation, at relatively short intervals, of prayer – liturgical or personal – with work, meals, recreation, reading. The day is broken up into short units allowing no long stretches for work or any other occupation. Constantly we are being called back to prayer. This too is an essential feature of the charism. Words cost nothing and we can tell ourselves so often that we live a life of prayer that we convince ourselves of its truth. In reality, to live a life of prayer costs everything and fidelity to a strict horarium will go a very long way to defraying the cost.

Teresa lived in a period of liturgical impoverishment and her Constitutions witness to it. She saw nothing odd in ordaining that Lauds are to follow straight on from Matins, somewhere between ten o'clock and half-past ten at night. Prime, Terce, Sext and None are grouped together and recited before Mass. Vespers are celebrated at two o'clock in the afternoon and, in Lent, at eleven in the morning! Even so, Teresa herself held Choral Office in high esteem. She reacted to the elaborate, long drawn out liturgies of the time and devised a simple form of recitation, prayerful, with pause, that aroused devotion in those who heard it. The Canonical Hours in her day were weighty and she was concerned that her nuns should not be overburdened with more. One of the motives – and a very strong one – behind her resolve not to accept endowments for her foundations, was precisely to avoid the burden of weighty suffrages imposed by the patrons. When abbeys and monasteries were social institutions, patronised by the rich and powerful and, as an historian neatly expressed it though in reference to another age, 'carrying more conscripts than volunteers,'[3] the celebration of Mass and the Office was seen as a function to be performed efficacious in itself, regardless of the dispositions of the celebrants. Therefore, the more Masses and the more elaborate and longer the Offices the better.

Teresa's spirit was very different. Her stress was always on the interior disposition and this called for simplification. Moreover, her nuns must have time for earning money and, of course, for hours of silent prayer. When circumstances forced her to accept endowments she did her utmost to guard against the disadvantages that tended to accrue. We hear her pleading for understanding from a patron:

> My idea was that chaplains should be obliged to sing Mass on festivals, for that is laid down in our Constitutions, but that the nuns should not be bound to sing, for their Rule allows them either to do so or not . . . I beg you to leave them free when they feel the necessity.[4]

And again:

> There is one thing, I think, that is troubling the community a good deal and which will bear very hard on them - namely, having Mass said before the High Mass, on festivals, especially if there is a sermon . . . [5]

We ourselves are blessed to live in a time of liturgical renewal, rich in insight. We have welcomed a revised and shortened breviary in the vernacular. The reduction in length has enabled us to celebrate the different Offices at their appropriate time throughout the day. Furthermore, we are able to conform with the general instruction that the Mass and major Hours are to be sung when possible, but with the simplicity and interiority that Teresa desired. It would seem that the present form of the Divine Office is ideal for the Teresian way of life, allowing for a truly intelligent and prayerful celebration.

As Carmelites, we are bound to Choral Office. We are not at liberty to decide that, as a community, we will, regularly, recite one or some Hours privately. Inevitably, individual sisters, by reason of their duties, may be obliged to miss a Little Hour. Nevertheless, our obligation to celebrate the whole of the Divine Office in common, must be taken very seriously and the day with its round of work, arranged with this in view. As far as individual sisters are concerned, each one must desire to be in choir with the community and be reluctant to seek exemption: to complete work, for instance; to carry on a conversation in the parlour; for minor physical ailments. Always, the celebration of the Divine Office has been considered the sacred obligation of nuns and monks. It is their *work* in and on behalf of the whole Church and, indeed, of the world – *Opus Dei, Officium.*

Work is often laborious, and calls for great sacrifice and we must be prepared for this in our 'work'. We can recall how Thérèse of Lisieux grasped the meaning, the inestimable spiritual value of the daily round and its importance to the Church. She gave her utmost right to the end. Sick, exhausted, she would strive to be as she said 'at my post'. A difficulty we have to reckon with is that the consequences of a lack of generosity regarding attendance at the Office are not observable. If a nurse fails to maintain night duty there are obvious consequences and the same goes for the ordinary obligations in the social order. What, in faith, we have to realise is that there are consequences, and serious ones if, for instance, because we are feeling tired or emotionally upset and longing to creep into bed, we ask to stay away from Office. There are consequences on the community level too. Nothing is more helpful and stimulating for a community than general fervour – each one aware of her obligations and determined to fulfil them: in choir first thing in the morning and last thing at night. Whereas frequent absences – even when wholly justified as must be at times – affects the morale of the whole. Strong motivation will grow through reading and reflection on the Church's understanding of liturgical prayer. The Divine Office is bigger than ourselves. Our own participation may seem poverty-stricken to us, but provided we are doing our best, our little curl of incense is caught up in the great column of prayer rising continually from Jesus and his Church. But we must give of our best both at the corporate and personal level. It will mean careful preparation both remote and immediate, making use of the talents and resources available, regulating the manner of reciting or singing accordingly.

On no account, I think, should they sing until there are more of them, for, if they do so, they will bring discredit to us all.[6]

We should not begrudge a reasonable amount of time for preparation of texts and their execution. As regards immediate preparation, this means ensuring that our books are well marked. What is more, and most importantly, we must direct our minds and hearts to this sacred duty. Warning bells, rung well before the actual summons to choir, are a great help if properly heeded. These bells tell us that the time has come for us to lay aside our work and other occupations and turn our minds to prayer. An attitude of mind content to be there just on time, that goes on working until the last minute, is hardly proper to our contemplative vocation whose priority is prayer.

We are human. God asks of us our reasonable service and there will rightly be exemptions that are wholly in accord with God's will. For instance, it would seem wise for the sisters to enjoy a monthly day of solitude and a private retreat with exemption from Choral Office; and perhaps, during the community retreat, for one of the Little Hours to be celebrated in private; and there may be other similar occasions when the prioress judges exemption fitting. However, what seems contrary to our charism, with its obligation to Choral Office is that for a whole day the monastic choir is silent, still less for several days at a time. Surely only some unavoidable mishap, such as sickness, could justify such a thing. Otherwise it could only occur where there is a lack of appreciation of the importance of the *Opus Dei* and the seriousness of our obligation.

This routine, this daily round of prayer and work, of obligations small and great embody the gift of ourselves to God. How else can we give ourselves? We give God what God asks, not what we decide to give; and how can we doubt that God asks of us precisely this round of unspectacular, maybe downright dull, duties? Everything depends on the love with which we do them, as Thérèse would insist.

CHAPTER SIX

Eremiticism in the Teresian Carmel

St Teresa's understanding of eremiticism

It is beyond question that the Teresian Carmel is life in community. Teresa's nuns live together, share their resources and are dependent on one another for everything. Moreover, they celebrate Mass and the round of the Liturgical Office, and take their meals together. Yet Teresa herself goes beyond the cenobiticism of St Albert's Rule, ordaining that the sisters should all meet twice a day for recreation, and she attached great importance to this practice. Presumably, when planning her Reform, she could have taken an opposite course and stressed the eremitical character of the Rule. This she did for the community as a whole, by a strict, carefully protected enclosure, but within the solitude of enclosure, she is more flexible. For her, relationships had irreplaceable value. We find no hint in her writings that she saw the introduction of two periods a day in which the sisters could talk together, as an innovation, still less a mitigation. On the contrary, she confidently affirms that her nuns were living the Rule in all its perfection. She relates with satisfaction, the reaction of the General of the Order, Fray Juan Bautista Rubeo:

> He was glad when he saw our way of life; for it gave him a picture, however imperfect, of our Order as it had been in its early days; and he was able to observe how we were keeping the Primitive Rule in all its strictness.[1]

In Teresa's Constitutions the pivot of the Rule remains unimpaired:

> All of that time not taken up with community life and duties should be spent by each sister in her cell or hermitage designated by the prioress; in sum, in a place where she can be recollected . . . By withdrawing into solitude in this way, we fulfil what the Rule commands that each one should be alone. No sister, under pain of a great fault, may enter the cell of another without the prioress' permission.[2]

And, under the same token of an obligation to solitude, 'Let there never be a common workroom'[3] (an almost universal custom in monastic life). The 'Great Silence' ordained by the Rule, stands intact:

> . . . the bell is rung for silence at eight o'clock, and the silence is kept until after Prime the following day. This silence shall be observed with great care.[4]

Then follows Teresa's own strict, but humanly balanced, rule of 'daytime' silence. For all that a Carmelite lives in community, she will spend a great deal of time alone or, if not alone, in silence. Ultimately, however, physical solitude must yield to the demands of community:

It is here, my daughters, that love is to be found – not hidden away in corners but in the midst of occasions of sin; and believe me, although we may more often fail and commit small lapses, our gain will be incomparably greater. Remember I am assuming all the time that we are acting in this way out of obedience or charity: if one of these motives is not involved, I do not hesitate to say that solitude is best . . . [5]

and, we may add, according to her mind and to the mind of the Rule, the 'home' of the Carmelite. We have a serious obligation to choose solitude whenever it does not conflict with service to the community.

In order to achieve a proper balance between the communal and eremitical aspects of our way of life, a balance essential for the authenticity of the charism and its effectiveness in exposing us to God's incessant sanctifying action, we need to grasp what St Teresa means when she asserts: 'The whole manner of life we are trying to live is making us not only nuns but hermits . . . '[5] To be alone with God alone is to be detached from self, with mind and heart directed to pleasing him only, and this demands asceticism, purification and natural maturation. A person can live in physical solitude, follow a strict rule of life, pray, experience great devotion, or desolation, and remain basically egotistical and personally undeveloped, emotionally stunted. John of the Cross insists that we simply cannot of ourselves, divest ourselves of our egotism. God has to act both directly and indirectly. Other people are God's chosen instruments and we have an absolute need of them in order to mature emotionally, intellectually and spiritually and to learn how to love – our life's greatest task. Living in community affords us unparalleled opportunities. Teresa and John share a deep appreciation of the purifying, sanctifying effects of community life if lived as it should be lived. Both excel in showing us how to exploit its potential to the full whilst avoiding its pitfalls: Teresa principally in *The Way of Perfection* and John in his *Precautions and Counsels to a Religious*. To expose ourselves generously to the demands of community life, to refuse to shirk them in any way is to expose ourselves to God, allowing him to purify us through others, shatter our illusions with humbling self-knowledge, divest us of everything selfish and enable us to love others with a pure, mature, disinterested love.

We must bring the same wholehearted generosity and fidelity to the ordinances of solitude and silence. It is not a case of choosing to be with others when we want to be and retiring into silence and solitude according to whim. There is an asceticism involved in silence and solitude as in community living and this is especially true for some temperaments. We abide by the Rule whatever our preference. There will be many times when, harassed by the demands of community, we long to escape to our cell, and times when hurt, troubled and lonely, we want the company of others to reassure and comfort us; but, nevertheless, we suffer our little suffering in solitude, under the eyes of God alone.

If Teresa and John give us abundant instruction as to how to live this creative 'tension' between the communal and solitary aspects of Carmel, Thérèse of Lisieux offers a lived example of total fidelity, and the consequences of such a fidelity in her human maturing, her wisdom and sanctity. Understanding the meaning of solitude and being faithful to it, and at the same time forgetting self in the service of the community, enables Divine Love to bring to being our true personhood. 'That they may be one as We are one': persons in oneness – such is

Christian community. We are not a mere group, still less a herd. Each of us has to stand alone before God, totally responsible for her own life: her thinking, attitudes, decisions, actions. We cannot renounce this responsibility either in the name of obedience or of community. We shoulder this lonely responsibility at the same time as we 'commune' with others in New Testament fashion: humbly accepting guidance, formation, support; putting all our talents at the service of others. A true community is a work of grace and not a natural product, but the Holy Spirit awaits our own indispensable contribution.

> My soul is occupied. This refers to the soul's surrender of itself to the Beloved in the union of love, wherein it devotes itself, with all its faculties, understanding, will and memory to His service. The understanding is occupied in considering what most tends to His service, in order that it might be accomplished; the will in loving all that is pleasing to God, and in desiring Him in all things; the memory in recalling what ministers to Him, and what may be more pleasing to Him.[7]

It is to this surrender that the interplay of solitude and community is designed to bring us.

CHAPTER SEVEN

The Observance of Enclosure

Reading the Primitive Constitutions, one cannot but be struck by St Teresa's lengthy treatment of all to do with the observance of enclosure. Although she surrounds her convent with high walls and fences to separate the community from the outside world – a world, however, which it needs for its very existence and towards which it has obligations – relationship with that world remains inevitable. Three places are designed and set apart in the monastery for contact with outside: the choir, where a grille separates and conceals the community from the congregation; the turn-room; and the parlour.

The 'turn', or revolving drum for the transmission of goods, was built into the room reserved for the portress, hence 'turn-room' or just 'turn'. (I will hold to this usage in this book.) The parlour, designed for receiving and conversing with people outside, was divided by an iron grille which effectively prevented all physical contact. Turns and grilles were not in themselves a Teresian creation but a common feature in houses 'for people who live recollected lives,' as Teresa explained to the difficult Archbishop of Burgos. He it was who interpreted them as an expression of independence in regard to his jurisdiction.[1] We see her, when arranging foundations, sending ahead her male friends to set up the turns and grilles prior to the nuns moving in, and thus ensuring that strict enclosure would be observed from the outset.

Another point of contact with outside, albeit of a limited nature, is the sacristy. Here too, a turn was installed for the transmission of everything necessary for Mass; and whatever verbal exchanges with the chaplain were necessary, took place through the aperture of the turn. The confessional, as was the common practice everywhere, had its little grille covered by a curtain.

The prioress guardian of the enclosure

According to the Rule of St Albert, the cell of the prior lay at the entrance to the monastic settlement and in this way he supervised all that came into it and all that went out. In substance, he was protecting the solitude of his brethren. A house in a town suburb bears little physical resemblance to the Wadi-es-Siah, as does a small room in that house to whatever comprised the cell of a hermit, but in Teresa's mind there was identity. She assigns to the prioress the keys of all the entrances to enclosure including the parlours, in this way enabling her effectively to guard the solitude of her community. This simple expedient gave her full control of whatever entered the monastery or left it and also, of all contacts in the parlours. Today, as already remarked, we would find such surveillance unacceptable. We ensure that the keys are available to each and all and every sister is relied upon to be faithful to the letter and spirit of enclosure. This way of trust is always preferable but should the prioress decide, for whatever reason, to keep a close watch in this matter and withdraw the freedom that has become the custom with us, she is within her rights. What is more, if she has reason to suspect abuse or carelessness, it would be her duty to intervene in so important an area. If we are really earnest in our vocation and understand its demands if we are always to be 'there', in prayer, in heart, in intention and as much as possible in mind also, we shall know that, in our weakness, we need supporting structures to be completely faithful. The vision can fade from time to time, and with it strong motivation and this is when we find ourselves taking little liberties that, at the time, seem unimportant. Hence the necessity for the regulations that the wisdom of the community – under the direction of its prioress, acting at the highest point of its understanding of the charism – has established. As individuals but also as a community we have constant need to revitalise love for our vocation and must support one another to be perfectly faithful to what is our heart's deepest choice. Our weakness and natural longing for pleasure pull in another direction. The greatest expression of love we can show is to incite one another to go on wanting what we really want and be willing to pay the price. Only then can we be truly happy and fulfilled. The purity of the charism calls for the greatest watchfulness on the part of all in regard to an authentic observance of enclosure.

The parlour

Undoubtedly Teresa, in her enactments, was reacting to the situation she knew at the Incarnation and all the evils that ensued from indiscriminate relations with seculars. There, the parlours resembled salons, where entertainment was received and given – a welcome diversion in a frustrated life. We have to recognise too, that within her own culture, the measures she considered necessary, would not have caused the shock they do today. Taking all this into account, still, we would be unwise to think that her severe legislation has little to say to us and consider ourselves immune to the abuses she had in mind. We hear her:

> No nun should be seen with her face unveiled unless she is with her father, mother, brothers or sisters, or has some reason which would make it seem as appropriate as the cases mentioned.

Further, another nun must always be present to hear what goes on and must warn the sister if the conversation should take a worldly turn.² Until the end of the nineteenth century, even in Great Britain, a 'respectable' young woman would be accompanied by a chaperone and in Teresa's Spain, veiled women were no unusual feature. Clearly, flirtatious gallants, or any others seeking entertainment from the 'charming' nuns, would be quickly deflected by these measures, and this was Teresa's purpose. It was her way of limiting visitors (close relatives apart) to serious-minded people who would approach the nuns in truth, that is, as women dedicated to prayer. Teresa wanted to abolish, not only 'worldly' talk but also long conversations of a merely social nature; by this she means conversation centering round what was, in her day, of such paramount importance – honour, prestige, pride in noble, pure blood and high family connections – together with everything that, given an honest appraisal, would class as gossip. Women dedicated to living with God alone, with duties towards the community, have neither time nor energy to spend in useless conversations. She ordains that, as soon it is realised that the visitor wants nothing else, the visit must be broken off. The vigilator (or chaperone) must enforce this should the sister demur.

Today, we no longer confront our visitors from behind a grille, still less with faces veiled, nor are we chaperoned. Yet the question we must always ask ourselves and answer with honesty is, whether without these inhibiting external factors, we remain truly faithful to the purpose they were intended to serve. Today we have first and foremost to be our own monitor, but, as already said, we need the example and support of one another. After all, we joined the community in order to be helped towards our high ideal.

Have we not to admit that we have known abuses: visits to the parlour encroaching on prayer, or used as a place for gossip? Surely we have heard the jibe: 'If you want to know the the latest news of the diocese, go to an enclosed monastery.' If there is truth in this, then most certainly we need to ponder the mind of Teresa and examine our conduct severely. The responsibility in great part lies on the individual, who must decide whether or not it is wise for her to receive a particular visitor and she must know the reason for her decision. Likewise, she must honestly examine herself after a period in the parlour, as to the benefit derived by herself or, hopefully, by her visitor. This whole issue reveals the need, not only for a deep understanding of the vocation and a willingness to face its exigencies, but also, for self-knowledge. Too easily, lacking self-knowledge, we can be 'using', or perhaps better, 'abusing' people outside to satisfy our own needs: relieving the monotony of the enclosed life; seeking an affirmation from visitors that we are indeed wise, spiritual women, a fact which our community seemingly fails to appreciate. Not infrequently, visitors are predisposed to endow a contemplative nun with an aura of holiness and foolish we are if we take their admiration seriously.

We may have to look closely at the degree of our conviction in the efficacy of the purely contemplative vocation and maybe we shall discover that what we are looking for in some of our contacts is the assurance that we are 'doing something', are of some apostolic benefit. This anxiety, often unrecognised because we are accustomed to hearing and ourselves affirming our conviction in the power of a life of prayer, is more common than we like to admit. We have everything to gain and nothing to lose by facing it squarely. We must be true to the vocation God has assigned to us and believe that it is through fidelity to it that we love others and help them. Our contacts in the parlours, the turn, and maybe the sacristy, now that the material restrictions have been removed, can, in the name of charity and Christian witness, lead us to step outside our own vocation. We are not apostolic sisters; the witness proper to them is not proper to us. Our witness must be that of enclosed nuns and 'not merely nuns but hermits', given up to prayer for the world. Courtesy, kindness, restraint in speaking when merely carrying on business; these should mark our witness. The fact that seculars feel closer to us, enjoy us more when we step outside our limits, matters not at all. To divest ourselves of our identity as Carmelites as if we were ashamed of it and to adopt a worldly stance in order to please others is indefensible. It is dealing them debased coinage. Yet timidity, narrow-mindedness, still less churlishness are even more so. We can find in Teresa's writings many references to what she expected of our behaviour towards seculars. She was renowned for her delightful way with people and she wanted us likewise to be pleasant and gracious so that people like talking with us and are attracted to our outlook on life, the values we cherish and so be drawn to imitate them.[3]

We have a special duty of love to our close relatives but even so, we must make sure that we really have 'left' them. Visits from parents and close relatives who cannot understand the vocation and are unable to accept that their daughter or sister has embraced it, offer a particularly painful challenge. To maintain one's identity and values as a Carmelite, to resist the efforts of our dear ones to control us and our conduct, can be very painful indeed and we need to support ourselves with Our Lord's uncompromising words: 'One who loves father or mother more than me is not worthy of me.'[4]

The portress dealing at the turn

Considerable space is given in Teresa's legislation to the duties of the portress, the sister commissioned to answer door bells and do business at the turn. She was responsible for buying supplies and for selling the handwork of the sisters. Teresa stresses that the prioress must ensure that the person selected is 'reliable'. Again, we find Teresa insisting on a surveillance which would be foreign to us today. Nevertheless, in all our business dealings, and with the chance callers at the turn, good judgment is called for. A judgment founded (as indicated earlier in this chapter) on a thorough understanding of and love for the vocation to prayer and solitude. The same dangers, the same cautions apply here as in the parlours. Writing of the portress of the newly-founded convent of Toledo, Teresa remarks with satisfaction

> ... she has very little to say for herself at the turn. Tell her [the prioress]) that she should leave her there, for that is a great virtue in the portresses of our convents. Here I have forbidden our portress, Alberta, to say a word.[5]

No doubt the special circumstances of those days induced such a stricture and, as such, is not imitable but merely an indication of the whole thrust of Teresa's thought concerning the silence and seclusion in which her nuns should live. It is likely that, today, the duty of 'being on the turn', answering the phone and so forth, is shared by several sisters. The same discretion born of sound judgment and appreciation of the vocation must govern the conduct of the sacristan and all other officials whose duties involve them with seculars. Modern times with their various forms of communication, present their own challenge, not least, the telephone and fax. No one can legislate minutely for their use, the principles expressed in Teresa's first legislation remain unchanged and must be applied in every instance as we have tried to demonstrate.

Exits

Undoubtedly, need for exits from the enclosure abound in our day. There is no escaping from them. Always we can be confident that when circumstances force us into them we can count on God's help and that nothing will be lost. But we have to be sure that circumstances are really intractable, that we have carefully examined the matter to see if ways can be found to avoid them and not too readily assume the contrary. At this point it may be opportune to raise the question of exits for shopping and our means of transport. It is worth noting that, in this context, we are faced once again, with a choice of the special Carmelite emphasis on total prayer, involving silence and withdrawal, over an expression of religious poverty such as availing ourselves of public transport or walking through the streets. Is it not incumbent on each community, in its own situation, to appraise how best it can sustain this choice in our everyday situation: obtaining supplies, mailing letters, dealing with the bank, health care? Surely a thorough grasp of the charism and Teresa's mind will lead us to do our utmost to finds ways and means whereby these demands can be met without a sister having to leave enclosure. An obvious thing to do is to employ a suitable person to act for us. Ultimately, it is our attitude that matters. What is to be deprecated as contrary to the charism of Carmel is to consider that routine excursions outside the monastery are to be considered today as part of an authentic life-style, to be exploited to form contacts and bonds with the local people who can then detain us and chat to us freely. Surely we must be consistent. Our fundamental attitude must remain the same as when we deal with externs from within the enclosure. The more unusual exits – stays in hospital, for instance – cannot be circumscribed in the same way. What is discussed here is precisely what could be frequent, maybe daily, exits.

Our own need of friends outside the monastery

So far we have considered our duty as hermit-nuns to avoid unnecessary contacts and at the same time to recognise that we have serious obligations of love towards people outside our enclosure. It is equally important for us to acknowledge that we ourselves need the support, enlightenment, and emotional comfort that others can give us. Moreover, we must not be afraid of genuine, intimate friendships with either sex. Such friendships are not merely to be tolerated but positively encouraged. Experienced in the context of silence and enclosure, they are inevitably accompanied by pain and entail discipline and sacrifice. If we value the friendship sufficiently, we will be willing to pay the price. Consecrated chastity, the surrender of our capacity to love to God, will most easily come to flower in the context of warm, human relationships. Sustaining and personally developing friendship can grow out of the hard ground of sacrifice.

All this calls for abandonment and the trust implicit in our vows – that, in surrendering our freedom to choose for ourselves, to look ourselves to the satisfying of our needs – Divine Love will take care of everything and ensure that, in fact, we want for nothing that would bring us closer to God. We may be fortunate in our former relationships which continue after we have entered the monastery. We may have to wait and look to God to send us the friends we need but this means being open to recognise one if sent. If we do not get the friend or the friends we feel we need we must simply believe that, at least for the present, we do not need them and that it would not be good for us to have them. Perhaps we are being invited to give closer attention to our companions in the monastery and value more the diffuse but staunch and faithful friendship they afford us. What matters is a realistic acknowledgment that we are not self-sufficient either as individuals or as a community. We need others as they need us.

The fact that this is an area open to abuse must not deter us. Something has to be risked for every great value. When it is a case of a really intimate relationship particularly with overtones of sexuality, it is wise to take into our confidence a person whose discretion and spirituality we can trust. We are never so blind as when our emotions are powerfully involved. We can recall St Teresa's self-reproach in refusing to heed an older sister warning her of the destructive nature of a friendship. She was too involved to hear. If our determination to give ourselves to God is fixed, then, early on, before our emotions get out of hand, we should seek another's support and guidance. The proper person would be the prioress, or novice mistress in the case of a sister still in the novitiate. Hopefully, these will have the openness to the Spirit to discern if this friendship, involving no doubt, pain, disturbance, struggle, is likely to help the sister to integrate her sexuality and come to sexual maturity which will, of course, mean a greater capacity for loving God and the neighbour. Hopefully, they will not dismiss it out of hand. What must always be borne in mind – and is, in fact, easily overlooked maybe because it is 'dangerous' – is that our emotional development is just as important as our intellectual growth. Some outside contacts are essential for this development.

The choir

St Teresa was concerned that her nuns, when in choir, celebrating the Mass and the Hours, be heard and arouse devotion by their devout praying and singing, but she did not want them to be seen. A view held today is that Carmelites should not only be known to pray but be seen to pray and therefore the sisters, at least for Mass, even though together in a reserved place, should visibly form one praying community with the people. The two hours of mental prayer likewise should take place in such a way as to be observed. A wise change? We might question the underlying motive. Is there a lack of conviction about the value in itself of the hidden life of prayer, a conviction held for centuries and which is indeed the very essence of the charism? Undoubtedly, today we are under heavy pressure, often from the noblest quarters and for noblest motives, to 'show yourselves to the world'; the world needs to see; you must share your life of prayer in a way the world understands, and so we become too concerned with an external, visible witness. Maybe this plea finds a ready compliance in our anxious hearts simply because, today perhaps more than ever, our particular vocation of hidden, silent prayer with nothing whatever to show for it, and maybe experienced as a 'nothingness', calls for enormous faith.

What we may not realise is, that in our concern for the external witness, for a manifest sharing of our life of prayer, we are weakening its efficacy and unconsciously changing the charism. There are many monastic communities and other forms of dedicated contemplative life today whose tradition and\or charism positively embraces this external apostolate of prayer. Teresa's Carmel has the distinction of being absolutely single-mindedly contemplative with no external apostolate. We must recall once again that our origins lie in the desert; our spirit is wholly eremitical. Our hours of silent prayer encapsulate in a special way our 'solitude', alone with God alone. Surely it is then, above all, that we need to be unobserved, able to enter as deeply as we can into this solitude. This desire for hiddenness is not self-indulgence, it is a need God puts in our hearts in order to draw us profoundly in faith into the depths of God to receive the outpouring of Love for the world. Changes that in any way inhibit this fundamental orientation, that, in fact, demands great attention and spiritual and psychic energy, are surely a betrayal, however innocent, of the very essence of the Teresian Carmel?

CHAPTER EIGHT

Friendship Among the Sisters – I

Within the title of this chapter is a confident statement of St Teresa's desire for genuine friendship to exist among the sisters of her community. We have seen how much, throughout her life, she valued the supportive, formative power of friendship and we can expect her to highlight its importance within her small band. However, the friendship she has in mind must exist and be cultivated within the austerity and silence of the desert of Carmel. Anthropologists tell us of woman's role in some primitive nomadic tribes, of carrying from camping ground to camping ground the embers of the fire that formed the centre of communal gatherings, with its comforting warmth and the reassuring circle of light it cast in the darkness all around warding off predators. Similarly, the gentle fire of warm, tender and steadfast relationships must never be allowed to die out within our community but constantly be fanned anew, affording comfort, encouragement and security. A blend of austerity and warm affection must be considered absolutely essential to the charism

... all must be friends with each other, love each other, be fond of each other and help each other.[1]

69

For not a few, awakening to that recognition of the importance of relationships in human development, there seems to be an innate contradiction between the highly structured monastic life with its strict rule of silence, and the fostering of friendship at any depth. This recognition leads to the conclusion that the structure and the silence must relax if more than lip service is to be paid to the notion of friendship. Considering the tradition of interpretation into which many of us entered, this is not to be wondered at. Far from fostering intimacy there seemed to be a deliberate intent to guard against it. Courtesy, kindness, friendliness, these undoubtedly were there but intimacy was not unless it were with the prioress, otherwise it was considered altogether dangerous and contrary to the detachment Carmel demands. We can confidently assert that this tradition, inspired no doubt by zeal for the integrity of the charism, was in fact alien to the spirit of St Teresa. A thoughtful examination of the legislation by which she structured the life, reveals that she positively catered for genuine friendship, whilst leaving eremiticism unimpaired. Fidelity to this structure (allowing, of course, for wise adaptations) enables us to gain its blessings which, as well she knew, make possible a more profound eremiticism, to live alone with God.

All sincere relationships, and these cannot exist without love, increase our self-awareness, expand our consciousness and ground us in a proper self-esteem which, in its turn, enables us to forget ourselves, frees us to look more steadfastly at God and the needs of others. In other words, our capacity for God is deepened. Emotional isolation, the sense of being important to no one and cherished by no one, is likely to be crippling, encouraging self-preoccupation and self-protectiveness as well as a spirit of mistrust.

A human person cannot expand properly without the consciousness of being loved by others, at least to some degree. To know that one is deeply loved by another, especially by someone who truly loves God, is a great gift from God and a powerful means for progress.

Recreation

Two periods a day for the sisters to come together – 'to converse on whatever topic pleases them . . . '² – was the principle means Teresa offered for fostering friendship within the community. It was intended also that these periods would provide relaxation and afford enjoyment. What Teresa seems to have taken for granted – namely, that meeting together to talk in what was otherwise a silent, concentrated and focused day, would, generally speaking, be refreshing – cannot be taken for granted today. It is important for us to distinguish between the dual purposes of the twice daily period of 'recreation': the fostering of warm relationships which consists in getting to know one another and giving and receiving mutual support and needful relaxation. There may well be times when the two fuse happily, and perhaps for some, most of the time, but not for all, at least not adequately. Conversation, the effort to listen and to communicate can be a costly self-giving bringing its own fatigue. Failure to make the distinction and, quite logically, maintaining that recreation is meant to be recreating, can easily lead to a neglect of the first aim, the simple labour of conversing lovingly with our sisters. Daily conversing together is part of our Rule, something God specifically asks of us. Undoubtedly St Teresa herself recognised the need for relaxation even when life was simpler and less stressed. She asks those with a talent for entertainment to put it to good use for the enjoyment of the community[3] and there has always been a tradition of home-made entertainment. Care must be taken though, lest in concentrating too much on entertaining, we minimise the importance of simple talking together.

Distinguishing the two aims Teresa had in mind in her legislation could result in our assigning one of the two periods precisely to personal relaxation, a silent free time in the middle of the day when sisters can rest, walk or do whatever helps them. This would leave us with no excuse for not giving our best at the hour devoted to the community. This would seem to accord more with the Teresian spirit than a rigid adherence to two periods of communal conversation which could, in fact, defeat both aims. Of course we recall how Thérèse of Lisieux and many others before and after her, insist that we go to recreation not for our own pleasure but to give pleasure to others. Yes, a thousand times yes. But there still remains the need for personal relaxation and maybe it is the most generous, those who constantly expend themselves, who have the greatest need. As individuals we do not claim it as a right and make no demands, but as members of a community we should endeavour to provide it for one another. If it is not catered for, there is the danger of sisters getting over-stressed, and maybe, only half-consciously perhaps, finding compensation in undesirable ways.

There is nothing in Teresa's legislation to suggest that she intended the recreation periods to be anything but spontaneous and informal. Many anecdotes bear this out. The strict formality many of us knew in our earlier days – the hierarchical seating, the multiple 'don'ts', the constant supervision – imposed constraint and debarred intimacy. To give an example: one of the axioms constantly voiced and carefully observed was that no one must say anything to her neighbour that she would not be ready to say to the group. There are not a few instances where authentic sayings and practices of St Teresa have been taken out of their own quite particular context and made into quasi law. Originally she envisaged her communities as small, not more than thirteen in number, and it is just possible for such a small group to communicate and relate as a whole. 'All must be friends.' Within a small, select band, a high degree of friendship could exist between each one, but once the original number is exceeded – it was Teresa herself who raised it to twenty-one – this becomes virtually impossible. It is doubtful if the saint ever thought this through; she says expressly of proper intimate friendships: 'Where a convent is large I should like to see many friendships of that type . . . '[4]

It is clear from Teresa's writings in general but most especially from her letters, that things were far from ideal in her first Carmels and relationships were often difficult and strained. In real life, just as much in Teresa's own day as in our own, building community, learning to love is a laborious business. The period of recreation is the occasion when we give ourselves up generously to this labour. 'All must be friends.' The word 'friend' covers a great range of intimacy and we must be realistic. In no way need the friendship Teresa, or anyone else, expects us to cultivate be of the deepest intimacy. That would be impossible. The key word is 'real'. This means that we work to give ourselves to others, not just in objective service but in sharing what is appropriate of our thoughts, our interests, our outlook on things, and at the same time we are open and ready to learn those of others. We do not begrudge our sisters the full hour but show them that it is a pleasure to be with them.

> Although you may be very sorry if all your sisters' conversation is not just as you would like it to be, never keep aloof from them if you wish to help them and to have their love. We must try hard to be pleasant, and to humour the people we deal with and make them like us, especially our sisters.[5]

Love demands that we take a genuine interest in each individual one without exception – after all, we are all she has got! – while avoiding intrusiveness. It is for the other to draw her boundaries and for us to respect them. Sensitivity, respect and kindness will make us quickly aware when our interest seems intrusive and unwelcome to another and likewise when it would be unwise, and unhelpful to reveal our personal concerns. Perhaps it is in this area of community relations above all others that good judgment, so desired by Teresa, is most called for, the instinct for knowing what is appropriate and what is not. Each of us must learn to trust, give of our real selves and relate from the heart.

Utterly deprecated as destructive of community, at least of a Carmelite community, is the view that everything must be out in the open with one another; each completely 'honest' with the other, saying what she really thinks. It holds that expressions of anger and other confrontational encounters are in order between members of a community. Such behaviour is likely to be nothing but self-indulgence at the expense of others, a retrogression rather than progress. Genuine love can only exist where there is deep respect for others and sensitivity to their 'otherness', their vulnerability, their needful self-protection.

Particular friendships

Something has been said already on the legitimacy and even desirability of healthy friendships, even of a very intimate nature, with those outside the monastery. Likewise must particular friendships between members of the community be defended.

No one has written with greater insight and sensitivity on mutual love within a community than St Teresa nor put such weight upon it:

> . . . we cannot be sure if we are loving God, although we may have good reason for believing that we are, but we can know quite well if we are loving our neighbour. And be certain that, the farther advanced you find you are in this, the greater the love you will have for God; for so dearly does His Majesty love us that He will reward our love for our neighbour by increasing the love we bear to Himself, and that in a thousand ways: this I cannot doubt.[6]

This love must be inclusive, embracing each one regardless of natural feeling. But what of those mutual affinities and attractions that are part of our human existence? Are they to be completely ignored? Insofar as they would diminish the inclusive love mentioned above, yes, but it must not be assumed that a response to them will necessarily do this.

For an earlier generation of religious, 'particular friendship' connoted something mysteriously evil and to be avoided. In our convent schools, pupils were not allowed to go about in twos. Whenever two were seen with heads together, someone stepped in to separate them. In Carmel, as already said, every precaution was taken to eliminate the possibility of a 'particular friendship'. If two sisters found themselves alone at recreation they could not speak until an authorised person came along or at least until they were joined by a third. The same restriction pertained on what were called 'license days' which probably began with St Teresa herself. At certain festal times, the silence was lifted and sisters visited one another to chat freely, but never just two at a time. It is difficult to think that this restriction derived from Teresa. True, in her letters we can find her advising a prioress not to allow a certain two sisters to talk much together but the reasons are clear; it does not follow that this represented her general practice. The very fact of the advice implies that such an embargo was not the norm.

The Primitive Constitutions as well as those of Alcala, specifically authorise intimate conversations between sisters.

> The Mother prioress may give permission should one Sister desire to speak with another so as to quicken the love each has for her Spouse or to be consoled in a time of some need or temptation.[7]

This clearly leaves the door to friendship wide open. It is strange that this point of legislation has been studiously ignored in communities otherwise dedicatedly adhering to the Teresian tradition. Teresa graphically portrays the sort of emotional relationship which has no place in Carmel.

> The devil sets many snares here which the consciences of those who aim only in a rough-and-ready way at pleasing God seldom observe – indeed, they think they are acting virtuously – but those who are aiming at perfection understand what they are very well:

little by little they deprive the will of the strength which it needs if it is to employ itself wholly in the love of God.[8]

Teresa goes on to describe the disturbing, destructive consequences of such involvements: over-sensitive reactions when the beloved is found fault with and inevitable unfairness in judgment towards the supposed offender, party-spirit, preoccupations with little presents, little services for the favourite, finding opportunities to talk together and thus infringing the rule of silence. How different a genuine friendship between Carmelites! In these the 'will is devoid of passion and indeed is helping to conquer other passions'.[9] Each helps the other to be truly faithful to all her obligations, small and great. Fidelity and the generous embracing of sacrifice, far from diminishing such a love, purify and enlarge it: 'When a convent is large I would like to see many such friendships of that type.'[10]

And, she continues:

> . . . when God has brought someone to a clear knowledge of the world and of its nature and of the fact that another world exists, and there is a great difference between one and the other, the one being eternal and the other only a dream; and what it is to love the Creator and what to love the creature [this must be discovered by experience for it is a very different matter from merely thinking about it and believing it] . . . what the Creator is and what the creature, and many other things which the Lord teaches to those who are willing to devote themselves to be taught by Him in prayer, or whom His Majesty wishes to teach – then one loves very differently from those of us who have not advanced thus far.[11]

Such genuine experience takes time; it is not likely to be there at the outset. It goes without saying that the spiritually mature can love very freely, very passionately without any danger to themselves or those they love. The same cannot be said of the immature. This does not mean that they are debarred from the friendship discussed until they are mature. Rather, the very struggle to love unselfishly can be a powerful means of spiritual growth – '... at first it [love] may not be perfect, but the Lord will make it increasingly so'.[12]

There can be no great, pure love without pain and sacrifice. We have to be convinced of its value, be willing to pay the price for it. It cannot be had cheaply. Its counterfeit is cheap enough and too many are satisfied with that.

We can recall with tender admiration the lonely fifteen-year-old Thérèse of Lisieux struggling bravely with her adolescent passion for the prioress, Mother Marie de Gonzague and the pure, lasting unselfish love she came to feel for this woman who caused her much suffering.

> From the very beginning of my religious life I had had to sacrifice my own inclination, for fear of getting attached to you in a wrong way – the merely natural attachment which a dog has for its master. The food of real love is sacrifice; just in proportion as you deny yourself any kind of self-indulgence, your affection for the other person becomes something stronger, and less self-regarding. How well I remember the violent temptations I had when I was a postulant, to make my way into your room, just for the pleasure it gave me; a crumb of comfort now and again! I had to pass your office at full speed, and cling tight to the bannisters ... [13]

Mother Marie well knew that Thérèse deprecated the flattery constantly offered to her as prioress, a flattery she avidly desired. Though she cherished no illusions about her, Thérèse really loved this gifted, attractive woman and her tender, compassionate loyalty deeply affected the older woman eventually winning her complete confidence to such an extent that she could confide to Thérèse her wounded pride and sensibilities following an election that did not return her to office, save at the seventh ballot.[14]

Equally instructive is Thérèse's fidelity in relation to her natural sisters living beside her in Carmel. Frankly they admit that it was she, the youngest, who set the uncompromising standard. Thérèse's heart was deeply bruised during the long years of detachment and, in particular, as she herself confided at the end of her life, she suffered acutely from the feeling that she had lost her 'little mother', Sister\Mother Agnes, and that she had all but forgotten her. For several years she worked as assistant to Sister Agnes and was frequently in her company but never once did she infringe the rule of silence. How moving it is to turn the pages of the *Yellow Notebook*, the recordings made by Mother Agnes of Thérèse's words during the last seven months of her life when all restriction between the two sisters was lifted. Thérèse rediscovered her 'little mother'. Here we find expressions of the deepest, tenderest love, poured out uninhibitedly. She 'needs' her 'little mother': 'You fill my last days with sweetness,';'You are my light,'; 'I would like you always to be with me; you're my sun,'; 'I cannot express what you mean to me.' Thérèse never tires of telling Agnes how much she loves her, asks her to sit where she can look at her constantly. 'When I hear the door open, I always believe it's you; and when you don't come, I'm very sad.' She wants to be fondled and kissed. 'Only in heaven will you know what you mean to me . . . For me you're a lyre, a song . . . ' Such impassioned words of love are flowing from a deeply purified heart, a heart taken up wholly in the love of Jesus, beating with his own love. Here is a 'particular friendship' of rare beauty.

We do not come to Carmel to find friends nor, indeed,

to find community as such. We come to give ourselves wholly to God and to make this a reality, we choose to live with others dedicated to the same purpose and within the same canonical way of life. But it should not surprise us that bonds of deep affection are formed between the members of such a group and that, within the general friendship, two sisters may find themselves drawn very closely together. We may not seek directly, still less demand a special friend but do well to remain open to the possibility should it be offered to us and embrace the asceticism involved.

Dining in a common refectory

Dining together is a precept of the Rule which St Teresa took over as a matter of course. It is not an option and belongs to the charism as an integral feature of our life in common. What may originally have come about for sheer convenience, has, through centuries of usage in monasticism, proved its value in fostering genuine community, and acquiring a quasi sacramental character. Easily the mind slips back to the morning Eucharist:

> . . . may the food we receive enable us to make our daily lives together a true living out of the bread we break together in each morning's Eucharist.

The sharing of food is a deeply human act expressive of family, of friendship, of mutual goodwill. Its symbolism works on us unconsciously. The social and community building character of meals in common could well be highlighted from time to time by a festal meal in which the silence is dispensed with.

This dining together, sharing a common table, had in Teresa's mind maybe an even greater significance coming as she did from a tradition that had neglected this point of the Rule. True, there was a common table but it was an expedient for the poorer members of the community who were dependent on it for their sustenance. The more affluent nuns could provide for themselves and we know that St Teresa had her own little kitchen. During the period when she was obliged to act as superior to her old community, one of her great preoccupations was to provide food for the large number of poor nuns who had not enough to eat.

Bearing this in mind, we can well understand Teresa's injunction in regard to charity: ' . . . if necessary, fast so that she may have your food',[15] a situation she intended should not arise within her own reformed band. All must share what was available with no privileges save for the sick and ailing and always they were to have preference.

In common with monastic custom in general, the community listens together to reading from the pulpit. The Rule ordains that the reading be of scripture. We must remember that the monks would not have their own copies of the bible and anyway probably could not read. They would be dependent on hearing it read aloud and where better than at the common meal? We do well to use this opportunity of listening together to any good form of literature: travel books, history, biographies.

Day after day, year after year, a great deal of useful reading can be absorbed as we eat our meal. An interesting book enjoyed in common is itself community building and a topic for recreation time. No less value has the reading that provokes disagreement. It is unwise and shortsighted not to exploit this educative possibility and well worth the trouble of finding suitable, enjoyable as well as instructive literature for reading aloud in the refectory.

It is a mistake to limit the notion of spiritual reading to those books which speak explicitly of God. Classics apart, a great deal of such 'spiritual' literature is third rate and hardly merits the name. God, we know, is revealed in the whole of creation, eloquent as it is of divine mystery, of divine love and purpose. Literature of quality that deals with natural phenomena, scientific facts, and above all, with human beings, their history, their emotions, their lives in general, is spiritual reading in an absolute sense and possibly gives us a far truer image of God than much 'God-talk'.

Teresa has more to say about our common meals but this will feature under a different heading in a later chapter.

Praying together: the liturgy

All of us today have ample opportunity for deepening our understanding of the Church's liturgy. This theological understanding is here presumed and our present intention is merely to stress the effectiveness of our communal celebration to create and nurture a truly Christian community. In a hidden but real way, through the objective power of the liturgy and especially of the Mass, each and all, in our weakness and defectiveness, participate in that Communion of Love which is the heart of reality, the Absolute

> that they may all be one; even as thou, Father, art in me, and I in thee, that they also may be in us, so that the world may believe that

thou hast sent me. The glory which thou hast given me I have given to them, that they may be one as we are one. I in them and thou in me, that they may become perfectly one . . . [16]

In any community existing around an altar, under the sacred ministry of the bishop, there is manifested a symbol of that charity and unity of the Mystical Body, without which there can be no salvation. In these communities, though frequently small and poor, or living far from one another, Christ is present. By virtue of him the one, holy, Catholic, and apostolic Church gathers together. For 'the partaking of the Body and Blood of Christ does nothing other than transform us into that which we consume'. We form such communities and what is said supremely of the celebration of the Eucharist, is true also of the Divine Office which is an extension of it.

We rightly draw encouragement from such affirmations but must always remember that the celebration of a liturgy, and especially of the Hours that conforms to the inner objective reality demands a constant unselfing, a 'labour', an *opus Dei*, nothing less. It demands sacrifice and asceticism on the part of each one and only in this way does it foster and express true communion, between ourselves, the whole Church, in the Trinity.

Many years ago, just after the close of the Vatican Council, the English hierarchy called a convention of the religious superiors from all the contemplative monasteries. One of the principle speakers was the Vicar for Religious of an archdiocese. For fifteen years he had regularly made the canonical visitation of contemplative communities. Before interviewing the sisters or even the superior, he made a point of being in the chapel during one of the Hours and this, he contended, enabled him to make

what proved to be an accurate assessment of the general
state of the community: its spirituality and its unity or
lack of it. He was attuned to the power struggles, frustra-
tions, self-display and self-assertiveness, inevitably but
sadly, finding expression in prayer in common, the discordancy reflecting the discordancy of hearts. And, of course,
by the same token, unity of heart, fervour, selflessness
even in what might be technically speaking a 'poor per-
formance'. Long experience does indeed show that in the
day-in-day-out and many-times-a-day attendance in choir
'the thoughts of hearts are revealed' and this should not
surprise or scandalise us. Rather, we should accept the
opportunity, the challenge that celebration in common
affords us to allow our egotism to be whittled down. It
calls for continual watchfulness: the glory of God must
matter supremely and our own feelings not at all. It means
listening attentively to the leaders, taking their time and
note, regardless of our own opinion or expertise and
trying our utmost to conform, to do our very best, to
carry out the instructions given us outside choir. And all
this in times of fatigue or emotional distress. It means
accepting the discipline and work of appropriate practis-
ing, in being taught and corrected, with no display of
sensitivity. It means really caring about the liturgy, coop-
erating with those whose function it is to promote it,
offering suggestions when asked for, giving our opinion,
looking up texts if required and undertaking whatever
trouble or work is demanded of us to create a worthy celebration.

A common effort towards so sacred an objective cannot
fail to foster strong spiritual bonds. We may be very conscious at times of the reality of our 'holy communion' but
we can be quite certain that, regardless of our awareness

or lack of it, that divine purpose which, we might say, is the very heart beat of the holy Communion of Love — the Triune God — is being brought to fulfilment.

CHAPTER NINE

Friendship Among the Sisters – II

Fraternal correction

There is a procedure of Albert's Rule which reads, in part:

> On Sundays, . . . or other days if necessary, you should discuss matters of discipline and your spiritual welfare; and on this occasion the indiscretions and failings of the brothers, if any be found at fault, should be lovingly corrected.

This mild prescription of Albert's Rule, we feel, in no way runs counter to the spirit of friendship St Teresa wanted to cultivate among the sisters of her community. When and by what spirit, we wonder, did this genial procedure get transformed into 'The Chapter of Grave Faults' with its accompanying penal code? It was not Teresa's own creation but, presumably accepting it as a matter of course as integral to the monastic life of the Order, she appended it to her own Constitutions.

Of its inclusion she writes:

> The punishment for the faults and failings in matters that were mentioned should be those penalties designated at the end of these

constitutions, according to the seriousness of the fault, since everything is set up in conformity with our Rule.[1]

Teresa's personal legislation closes with a section describing the relationship she wanted to see between the Mother Prioress and the sisters, a relationship of trust and intimacy such that every month, each would freely give her an account of her way of prayer so that she, the prioress, could guide her interior progress.[2] This must be seen in context, of course. At the time these Constitutions were devised, her sisters were still little more than novices and she herself was their prioress. We notice that it is a relationship similar to that between the novices and their mistress, who is instructed to treat her charges with compassion and gentleness.[3] All the more jarring then, are the appended chapters.

We cannot hope to enter fully into the mentality of earlier centuries. Evidently the sensibilities even of monks and nuns, were not offended by the infliction of corporal pain as punishment. What to us would seem cruel and personally degrading and unthinkable on the part of authority was at that time taken as a matter of course, arousing no strong reaction. Perusing the penal code we must bear in mind that in earlier times clerics, monks and nuns could not be tried in the criminal courts of justice even for such crimes as murder. They were referred to the ecclesiastical courts and, in the case of religious, those of the Order. The General of the Carmelites was surely not setting a precedent when he sentenced contumelious friars to service in the galleys. Penalties for faults could be very severe indeed. We are startled at the severity with which Doria, when Vicar Provincial of the Discalced, punished Mother Anne of Jesus and Mother Maria of St

Joseph, Teresa's most trusted daughters, for attempting to forestall his intention to make changes in Teresa's Constitutions. They went over his head and appealed to Rome and their appeal obtained a favourable reply. When Doria retaliated by threatening to wash his hands of the nuns, they surrendered. Mother Anne was, for three years, deprived of active and passive voice in chapter, confined to a cell and allowed communion only once a month. Mother Mary of St Joseph in her turn was deprived for two years of active and passive voice, confined for one year in a locked cell, forbidden to communicate with others by written or spoken word, or to assist at Mass, except on Sundays, and allowed to confess and communicate only once a month.[4] The two nuns seem to have taken all this in their stride and on completion of the period of penance resumed their tireless work for the Reform. The psychology that devised the traditional chapter of faults and penal code and could shoulder its application with equanimity is certainly not our own!

But, we still have to ask what benefits Teresa herself perceived in the chapter of faults and other similar corrective measures: the role of the zelatrix or monitor for instance? 'The monitors should take great care to notice faults, for this is an important office, and they should tell the prioress about them.'[5]

Undoubtedly, there was Teresa's deep concern to preserve the strict observance she had established. After all, relaxation was the norm in many religious houses and she herself had direct experience of the spiritual losses incurred. Her Reform was pulling against the current and needed constant watchfulness and firm resistance to any slackness. As already observed, we find her particularly heavy-handed in the case of faults committed in dealings with those outside: faults of 'worldliness'; getting involved with the besetting sin of the culture; concern for pure blood, rank, prestige, noble lineage, inheritances, money. We can understand how readily visiting relatives would engage in such matters and how easily a young sister, herself only recently 'immersed in such vanities', would be drawn into it. A 'listener' must always be present to warn her should she slip. If, after three warnings, she persists, then the prioress – and only the prioress – must be told. The penalty was severe. It is worth noting at this point, that, along with much that offends us, we find Teresa's moderate human touch. There is to be no 'telling tales'. If the sister corrected her fault nothing further would be said and the listener would keep it to herself.[6] Again:

> No nun should reprove another for the faults she sees her commit. If they are serious, she should admonish her privately in a charitable way. And if the nun after being told three times does not amend, the Mother Prioress should be told but no other Sister.[7]

Along with her zeal for maintaining an observance aimed at 'all perfection', Teresa saw the chapter of faults and all related to it as promoting humility.

> They should be very careful not to excuse themselves unless in matters where it is necessary to do so, for they will find much benefit in this practice.[8]

> The monitors . . . when ordered by the prioress, should at times reprimand the Sisters in public, even though this may mean that a younger Sister is reprimanding an older one. One is thereby exercised in humility. Thus the Sisters should not answer back even if they are without fault.[9]

What is the experience of those of us who for many years

lived within this system of correction? Could we say that it was, in fact, an effective instrument for preserving observance? Did it foster humility? These are crucial questions that deserve a careful answer.

Frequently, sisters, when questioned, admit that the very memory of the procedures provokes strong emotions. Others' reaction may be less vehement but nearly all admit to distaste. My own community, once the chapter of faults was abolished, chose to hold its discussions and chapter business of whatever kind away from the chapter room to avoid the 'atmosphere' of anxiety, suspicion and lack of trust which that room seemed still to hold. This negative response on the part of dedicated, fervent sisters is surely significant and points to the unsuitability, the inappropriateness of the former practice for our culture and times.

Now, to answer the questions posed above more specifically. The danger with the old system was that it concentrated on external behaviour and this could mean minutiae, such, for example, as to whether one held one's hands under the scapular when walking through the house or at other times; whether one was infringing the many little rules and regulations regarding meals.

Aware that details of behaviour were considered important, too much attention was given to them and much less to the formation of a deep interior life which, of course, it was intended these little practices should aid. Add to this the natural anxiety that one was under observation and was liable to be corrected publicly for infractions – which no one enjoys! True, a certain standard of 'religious behaviour' would be safeguarded but at what price and, one might add, of what worth? The only observance of value and one that serves the purpose for its creation is that which springs from deep conviction of its importance as a means to an end: the end is desired, the means are freely chosen. This must be our way today, whatever merits the older practices had in former times and different cultures. We will give far less attention to unimportant details. After all, many of the rules for 'religious deportment' that we were taught were largely the etiquette of Victorian 'ladies'.

One of the great traps of the 'old regime' was that of confusing 'behaviour patterns' with solid virtue: 'a Carmelite never does this, never does that'; 'a Carmelite should always'; 'she was a perfect Carmelite, never questioned a command, never infringed silence, never excused herself, always kept custody of the eyes and, of course, was never known to get angry or even show impatience'; 'Sister X never excuses herself, she is so humble . . . ' It is relatively easy to acquire behaviour patterns especially when one is young; it is very, very hard to become really obedient, really humble. The daily life was peppered with what were considered expressions of humility: kissing the ground when reproved, kneeling to the prioress, confessing one's faults in the refectory or in the chapter, performing 'dramatic' actions such as kissing the feet of the sisters, allowing them to walk over you as they entered the refectory and so on. We may never say that such practices bore no fruit. If they were carried out with love and a desire to humble oneself, as surely was the case with most sisters, they would, of course, as all acts of love, bring their own reward. It does not follow that such practices in themselves were pleasing to God, in conformity with Jesus' teaching. Leaving aside their inappropriateness to the point of revulsion, there was always the danger of pretence, of merely conforming – 'these things are done so I must do them or be thought wanting'. When imposed as penance they could arouse resentment and anger and seem degrading. Community life properly lived, requires no such artificial expressions of humility. It brims with daily opportunities: for learning what it means to be a servant with Jesus, truly lowly, gentle and humble of heart towards others; for overcoming our sensitivity; for holding back a swift rejoinder to a hurtful remark; for accepting to be passed over, content with any office, any household chores. What is more, as Teresa herself insists, true humility is the effect of light and love infused by God. We cannot acquire real humility, which is grounded in Truth but, as with all else, we do what we can, work towards it, open our hearts to receive it, show our desire to receive it by a loving humility with our companions.

What of fraternal correction? Taken for granted, as already quoted, is the Gospel precept regarding a grave fault of which we are aware. We protect our sister's name, warning her privately up to three times, and only if she does not amend do we speak to the one in authority. Taken for granted too are the apologies and forgiveness we offer to one another. For her part the prioress must not shirk the painful responsibility of correction, always with gentleness, aware of her own shortcomings and never speaking as if from a morally superior position. Automatic, indiscriminate correction can never be right. The golden rule must be the good of the other. When we see that a sister would not understand or would not be able to take a correction in a good spirit, to insist would do harm, fomenting bitterness and resentment, or at the least, leaving her with a wounded heart and confused mind. The weekly community meeting will provide a forum for community self-criticism and correction. Before discussing this important act, we must review other communal ways of asking and granting forgiveness.

First and foremost of these is, of course, the sacrament of Reconciliation. Unlike the other sacraments, the 'matter' and 'form' take place in the greatest privacy as the Church insists, but nevertheless, its essential communal character must not be overlooked. Our selfishness and lack of love, our 'No' to God, are not just a matter between ourselves and him but wound the whole community of the Church. Jesus is the great Amen, the unwavering 'Yes' to all God's promises, to God's eternal decrees of absolute love and fulfilment. There was never a 'No' in Jesus and therefore the Father was able to accomplish in and through Jesus all that the Father desired. Life in Carmel is ordained to uniting ourselves to this great Amen as did Mary with her 'fiat', to allow the divine waters of life to penetrate the world. The living waters are there in abundance: the well-spring opened up for ever, but human hearts block their flow.

We confess to God but also confess to the Church which we have wounded. Morning and evening, as a community, we make our examen. In the morning we recite together the Lord's prayer and in the evening the 'I confess . . . to you, my brothers and sisters . . . ' The hebdomadary as our representative prays for absolution: 'Whose sins you shall forgive they are forgiven . . . ' In the fullest sense this 'power' is invested in the ministerial priesthood but as representative of the whole Church. It is the risen Lord who utters them, proclaiming our perfect reconciliation with the Father, our at-homeness in him for ever; the good news to be communicated by each one of us to all by our thoughts, words, deeds. 'Loose him and let him go,' Jesus commands the friends of Lazarus standing by. We, by our forgiveness, our warm, open-hearted acceptance and love, loose the bonds of others, as others loose ours. Again, at the beginning of the conventual Mass, each one is invited to examine her conscience, confess and express her sorrow and then, all together, we receive absolution. Surely these communal confessions, petitions for forgiveness, and absolutions, are incorporated into the sacrament of Reconciliation. No doubt in many monasteries, as the confessor is not resident, the sacrament will be celebrated for all at an appointed time. St Teresa clearly envisaged this situation:

> She [the sacristan] should arrange that the hearing of confessions proceed in good order and, under pain of grave fault, she must not allow anyone to approach the confessional without permission unless to confess to an appointed confessor.[10]

This practice certainly highlights the communal character of the sacrament but possibly at the expense of freedom. It is the mind of the Church that the sisters enjoy not merely freedom but also genuine privacy in regard to the frequency with which they approach the sacrament. It remains absolutely their own responsibility before God.

The weekly community meeting

The community meeting, as far as possible held every week, is, when fully exploited, an incomparable means for building up community and true friendship, making possible a more penetrating grasp of what Carmel is meant to be, continuing the formation of the community. It is an effective instrument for maintaining proper discipline and purity of life-style. Various procedures are possible. The simplest and probably most frequent will be informal. The prioress may give the community information, express her concern at times over lapses she observes and exhort to the contrary and then invite others to speak. Even matters that in themselves are trifles must be allowed a hearing: for example, inconveniences or extra work caused by thoughtlessness and sheer ignorance. In a life of silence where recollection is the order of the day, without a lot of experience, it is impossible for each one to know the difficulties encountered by the various office holders and we should be glad to be informed of them. No one would knowingly cause another extra work and these observations can encourage thoughtfulness and care, as well as admiration and sympathy for one another.

A very important, wholly hidden expression of charity is a constant thoughtfulness for others in the offices they hold, trying to remember how they want things done and being careful to avoid adding in any way to their burden of work. True, there is merit in keeping to oneself the little annoyances caused by others' thoughtlessness or ignorance but, all things considered, it may be of greater benefit to the community as a whole, occasionally to make them known. Nor should we disdain the simple, honest admission of resentment at others' behaviour which can 'clear the air', and the community meeting is an appropriate forum. This is far better than allowing things to fester. It is taken for granted that all criticisms be of a general nature and that no one is singled out. This does not abrogate from the prioress' right to correct an individual publicly or order her to make known her transgression which may have been hidden. But this will be a very rare procedure and undertaken only after serious thought and in accordance with the golden Rule. No doubt, we will hear mention of faults of noisiness, untidiness and other little irregularities. The prioress may take up the observations made and develop them. More serious matters may be raised but usually in the form of a question and then a general discussion may ensue with profit to all.

This freedom to express opinions, offer suggestions and criticism – always with charity – in no way undermines the prioress' authority, which she may never abdicate. However, she herself can learn by listening to her community and the more they are challenged to think, really to listen to one another, the more are they likely to mature and grow in insight. We have to reckon with the reality that far more than we imagine, our judgment is emotional rather than rational. To voice our opinion in public and have others counteract it can reveal the weakness in our thinking – but only if we are prepared to listen and are not intent on defending our own position.

When one considers the old practice of chapter of faults at which, apart from accusing herself of her own faults, no one was allowed to speak unless invited to do so and all correction fell to the prioress whose opinion alone was heard, we can appreciate the spiritual and psychological value of such a free procedure. A prioress would need extraordinary wisdom and spirituality, possess abundant self-knowledge, to be immune to the perils in being the only confidante for complaints and criticisms. Almost inevitably, this situation leads to lack of trust among the sisters themselves, to partialities and not infrequently to an individual becoming a scapegoat. School children would despise such conduct as 'sneaking', 'telling tales' and, in itself, it is obnoxious. The good name of the community must be safeguarded and in certain cases, where harm to the community might be involved, there would be the obligation to inform the prioress if the sister herself refuses to do so. But everything is to be gained and nothing lost by a prioress letting it be known that she will not listen to criticism of others, but insist that the one making the complaint deals with it herself. A great deal of manipulation comes into play if the prioress allows tale-bearing. If the criticism is of a general nature then the sister herself can make it at the community meeting.

We build up our community in all sorts of ways, not least by silent example, but also by our words. Some ways have already been suggested but there are others, such as organised discussions, when an agenda is prepared and time given for research and reflection. Everyone must apply herself seriously to the topic. The prioress herself will be ready to animate and inspire her community and take the time to equip herself for this. She may invite other members of the community to talk on a subject of her or their own choosing and all should be ready to offer this service. As time passes the benefits of this weekly meeting will be seen and not least of these will be the implicit sense of security each one has in such an open atmosphere. There are no dark secrets, everything is above board, in the light as befits children of the light.

CHAPTER TEN

'Unoccupied' Prayer

Carmel's way of life is a whole. Its main components must
be embraced and lived without selection. Sacramental life,
liturgy, private personal prayer, community, solitude . . .
each has essential value and must be given its full weight.
Only by our wholehearted commitment to the whole, can
the purpose of Carmel be realised. Yet, if there is one element that can be said to embody or symbolise the essence
of Carmel it is solitary personal prayer. From the outset,
St Teresa ordained that a minimum of two hours daily be
set aside for private prayer. *The Life*, *The Way of Perfection*,
The Interior Castle as well as her minor works, all stress
the supreme importance of this solitary communion with
God. It was a Carmelite's 'business', her occupation, her
raison d'être. It has been said that it is above all by her
steadfast fidelity to these two hours a day that a Carmelite
is forged. In what way does this silent prayer embody the
whole meaning of Carmel? Intellectually, an educated
Christian will hold that salvation comes from God: 'Who
then can be saved?', the astonished disciples ask Jesus. His
answer is uncompromising:

> Jesus looked on them and said, 'With men it is impossible, but not
> with God; for all things are possible to God.'[1]

To be saved comprises the totality of that for which God in love has destined us, exceeding absolutely our natural powers. God must come to us and draw us to himself and we are assured that it is his gracious will to do so. That this is fundamental to the New Testament, no one would deny. Understood correctly, the sacraments are expressions of God's Self-gift to us in Christ: all is given, all is done for us, we have but to 'Take and eat', 'Come to me that you may have life', 'Come to me and drink'. We have not to provide our own worship. In the Mass we are given the perfect worship, the very surrender of Jesus. We do not, cannot, of ourselves atone, make reparation, put right our offences, but are given in the sacrament of Reconciliation the perfect atonement, the perfect reparation of Jesus. Sick and dying, we are not left dependent on our own resources, but in the sacrament of Anointing receive Jesus' comfort, his faith, fortitude and surrender to the Father's will.

However, the truth is difficult to integrate in such a way that it becomes our own truth by which we consistently live, running counter as it does to our natural understanding and natural urge to work for our own well-being and fulfilment. We forge our characters by the practise of virtue, strive to be genuinely good people, realising that no one can do this for us. As religious persons, it is natural for us to think in terms of merit, pleasing God with our efforts and good works and thereby ensuring his favour. Not infrequently, the celebration of the sacraments is seen as our 'good work', something we do for God; our attitude akin perhaps to that of our Jewish forebears as they performed their rituals. Yet Jesus undercuts this natural religious approach, showing us that union with God, which is our ultimate fulfilment, can be received only as pure gift; in no way can we bring it about or even merit it. For this we are helpless as babes-in-arms. Over and over again the point is made: 'Whoever does not receive the kingdom of God like a child shall not enter it.'[2] Divine love is unconditional: the son is received into his father's embrace and restored to full sonship simply by coming back; the shepherd goes off and risks his life to save the sheep incapable of saving itself; the workers of the last hour get the full wage. The deeply-rooted notion of earning, of merit and reward, is turned upside down by Jesus.

When our Christian faith assures us of God's dedicated love, we do not mean merely that God is good to us, looks on us with tender benevolence, always intent on our eternal happiness. Love involves the gift of self. Love is self-donation. God gives not merely gifts but his own self, and *is giving always*: 'My Father is working still, and I am working.'[3]

What else is this divine work but that of healing, purifying, transforming each one of us through the gift of God's self? Neither the Father nor Jesus, who always does what he sees his Father doing, rests from this work. It is, of course, the Crucified who reveals the full extent of this divine Self-expenditure, a total outpouring that holds nothing back. If we take this fundamental truth with all seriousness, then we realise that, as Christians, our inmost heart in relation to God, must always be receiving and that the only way we can 'serve' God, the only way we can 'give' to him is to allow him to serve us, to give to us.

The story of Martha and Mary vividly illustrates the point.[4] To understand that what is involved is an orientation of heart, a basic attitude in our relationship with God, we must note that it follows directly on the parable of the Good Samaritan. Jesus enters Martha's house and Martha does the obvious thing for a guest – prepares his meal. But her sister behaves differently. Instead of helping Martha which, after all, would be the charitable thing to do, Mary sits at Jesus' feet – to be fed by him, and this is the attitude that he commends, the better part. Mary's insight is correct. When Jesus, no ordinary guest, enters our house, he comes to feed us; we feed him by allowing him to feed us. Fed by him, loved by him, receiving him, then as Martha, we serve others with his own Self-expending love, but even so, our inmost heart must remain Mary, intent on receiving Jesus. Our precise vocation as Carmelites is to live this basic Christian attitude in its 'pure form', as we might say. We have no secondary aim, no pastoral ministry, no active service in the Church, no achievement: 'Why was the ointment thus wasted?'[5] Our lives are that ointment, 'wasted', poured out in love as we recognise the Self-squandering of Jesus and in him, the divine excess of love: 'To see me is to see the Father.'[6]

This is our ministry in the Church, rarely understood, rarely appreciated by others but, nevertheless, one of vital importance. The hours of solitary, 'unoccupied' prayer are the most powerful expression of this vocation and our most practical act of faith in God whom we know through Jesus as total Self-gift.

Human as we are, in common with everyone else, we eat, sleep, work, serve one another, talk, play, read, celebrate liturgy. This is God's will and whenever we are doing God's will we are praying: open to God, receiving God. But at least twice a day we leave every occupation aside and, as far as possible, the mental occupation that accompanies it, and set ourselves before God, exposed in our naked reality, undefended by the ritual of liturgy, planned meditation or techniques with which to maintain control; with nothing whatever to offer except ourselves and the desire to receive God's outpoured love. Apart from faith, such hours have no meaning, they are a waste of time but faith assures us that they are pregnant with significance, not only for ourselves but for the Church. We are offering God the very best opportunity for his divine action, inviting his purifying love to penetrate every corner of our being so that everything in us is transformed. Only then can we hope that each moment of our day, whatever its content, be most truly prayer, in fact, not merely in desire.

God's action, God's giving of himself during these hours of prayer, will not normally be experienced by the conscious mind and may afford little satisfaction, not even that of the assurance that we are really praying. What is more, it will reveal our spiritual indigence and shatter all complacency and this will demand on our part a humble trust. Over and over again we need to reaffirm our faith in God's unconditional love, unwavering in its attention to us, and ground ourselves on his fidelity, his word, not on how we feel, how it all seems to us. Prayer is essentially what God does for us; our part is to be 'there', wanting him to do all he wants, to give all he wants, and believing that he does so though we receive no sensible reassurance. How much easier it is to do things for God, to serve our sisters, nurse our sick, console and counsel another – these give us the satisfaction of being of some use, doing some good! How easy to evade this naked exposure to love and especially when prayer is arid and we are feeling upset, disgusted with ourselves and 'out of sorts'. But once we have grasped the importance – indeed the wonder – of this prolonged encounter, the hours assigned to it will be held sacrosanct, as belonging to God and not ours to dispose of. Only when it is evident, through the call of some indispensable duty, that God is here and now asking something else, will we forego prayer. A failure to attach the greatest significance to solitary prayer would seem to indicate a failure to understand the vocation as a whole.

The term 'unoccupied prayer' has been used instead of 'mental prayer', not merely to distinguish it from liturgical prayer or prayer in the broad sense of life lived directed to God, but also, and just as importantly, to imply that the emphasis is on the passive aspect of prayer, on God's activity not our own. We cannot deny that infused or mystical prayer, is the chief concern of Teresa and John. They touch on the earlier stages only so as to help us towards and clarify our understanding of the reality of infused prayer. Often enough, as inferred in an earlier chapter, minds have been confused by undue weight being put upon some psychological concomitants which, in fact, have relatively little significance. Infused prayer itself is an ineffable encounter with the living God. Teresa to some extent (for it must be admitted, she is not wholly convincing) and John most emphatically, warn us against the error. John is unequivocal: to seek 'experiences', 'favours', 'delights', to be over-involved with them, confines us to wandering round and round the slopes of Carmel without ever reaching the summit. The essence of mystical or infused prayer is nothing less than God's gift of God's own self and therefore, in itself, inaccessible to ordinary consciousness. Undoubtedly it can be accompanied by deep sensible peace and delight but is no less itself for their absence. God knows what is best for us. Some flowers reach their full glory only when nourished in rich soil with abundant water, while others wither in such conditions; dry, arid soil is what they need. God knows us individually and can be trusted to supply our every necessity. But one and all can draw profit from John of the Cross. He identifies infused contemplation with the 'dark night':

> This dark night is an inflowing of God into the soul, which purges it from its ignorances and imperfections, habitual, natural and spiritual, and which is called by contemplatives infused contemplation or mystical theology. Herein God secretly teaches the soul and instructs it in perfection of love, without its doing anything, or understanding of what manner is this contemplation . . . He prepares it for the union of love with God.[7]

The gift of God – understood literally – is offered to all without exception but, as both our saints sadly attest, so few prepare themselves adequately to receive him or accept the purification of Divine Love.

Our preparation

As Carmelites supported and instructed by a rich heritage of literature, we have little excuse for underestimating the generosity, wholeheartedness, earnestness and courage that must be expended to correspond with God's initiative, to be alert to his knockings, determined to say 'Yes' to every sacrifice. The very structure of Carmel is designed to simplify and direct our course towards God and God alone. Closer to our own day, Thérèse of Lisieux exemplifies one who took the straight path up the mountain and reached the summit. She knew little or nothing of the 'favours', the 'delights' of which the Spanish mystics write, but who can doubt that she received 'all God has to give', and was a true mystic who, within the last two years of her short life, attained and lived the state of transforming union or spiritual marriage? Her torment-ing doubts, darkness and trials of faith notwithstanding, she was mysteriously aware that this was so. How faith-fully she prepared, how generously and diligently she used all the graces and helps that life in Carmel offers, persevering in her simple, 'dry' hours of prayer, with no pretensions, basing herself far more on the Gospel than on mystical writers as such.

St Teresa set the time when the whole community would devote themselves to prayer. There is everything to be said for a fixed hour, with a formal beginning and ending. As a community we must support one another and not overestimate our spiritual strength and maturity but rather admit our weakness which would easily excuse us, were we left unstructured, from praying for an hour in times of discouragement and tedium. In the earliest days of the Reform, the sisters were free to pray in their cells but by the time of the Chapter of Alcala, twenty years or so later, all were obliged to be together in choir and the time had been changed from the hour preceding the night Office, to around five o'clock in the afternoon. We pre-sume experience had shown that both these changes ensured greater fidelity.

For not a few sisters, the close proximity of others and the inevitable physical restrictions it imposes hinders rather than helps recollection.

Those of us trained in the old custom know well how easily one became self-conscious about causing the slight-est physical disturbance, concentrating on stifling a cough, enduring cramp or an aching back! To keep move-ment to a minimum, it was the custom for all to kneel upright for the first period and sit only when the president gave the knock, kneeling again at a further signal. A prayer of endurance perhaps, and one could argue that cultivating physical stillness, no matter how painful, is important for contemplatives, but we are justified in asking if this, in itself, has anything to do with Christian prayer. The community has to reflect on its own particular situation and needs in order to decide what best helps sisters to give themselves up in freedom to a loving tryst with Our Lord. Individuals vary greatly and freedom of choice seems desirable in everything except the fixed hour. A really suitable hour must be chosen for prayer, preceded by a short period of preparation. We can be scrupulously faithful in our observance of the prescribed hours of prayer simply because they are prescribed but fail to grasp their centrality and significance. In fact, all the other points of the Rule converge on this one, are orientated towards it. To 'sandwich' the hour of prayer, to 'fit it in' between what are judged equally important exercises enjoined by the Rule, to cut corners, feel no exigency to ensure having a short period of preparation, to leave things to the last minute, to limit the time we devote to personal prayer to the minimum our Rule requires, hardly expresses the charism of Carmel and the mind of St Teresa.

> All that time not taken up with community life and duties should be spent by each Sister in the cell or hermitage designated by the prioress; in sum, in a place where she can be recollected and, in those days that are not feast days, occupied in doing some work.[8]

Presumably, on feast days, it is expected that she would give herself to prayer. However, we must be prudent in face of this expectation. From St Teresa's writings, both books and letters, we can infer that, for her contemporaries, prayer as often as not was a consoling occupation. She was well aware that it was not always so — and for some, rarely so. These she encourages never to give up,

> Whatever may come, whatever may happen to them, however hard they may have to labour.[9]

And:

> Let us not be discouraged, then, or give up prayer or cease doing what the rest do . . . [10]

However, the *Foundations* (Chap 5) supports the contention that, generally speaking, prayer was satisfying. She asks the question:

> What is the reason of the discontent which we generally speaking experience when for a great part of the day we have not been withdrawn apart and absorbed in God, although we may have been employing ourselves in these other matters?

Teresa draws the conclusion that not a little self-love is involved.

For various reasons, as has already been suggested in an earlier chapter, Carmelite nuns of today, with their educated, somewhat critical minds, are less likely as a normal thing, to experience prayer as delightful, once the initial phase is over. Nor, generally speaking, are they drawn to such devotional practices as the Stations of the Cross and recitation of the rosary, to which, no doubt, Teresa's contemporaries devoted time in the solitude of their cell or hermitage. Moreover, modern Carmelites have needs unknown to their sisters of old time, which must be met *if they are to become true contemplatives*, and time must be allowed for them. (We will return to this point later in the chapter.)

A further factor must be borne in mind: deep prayer,

whether in the light or in the dark, is an exposure to God, and the deeper the prayer, the more intense the exposure, so prudence is needed and, generally speaking, it is wise to limit it to an hour at one time. It is doubtful if deep prayer could be sustained for longer, whereas many hours can be spent in other forms of prayer such as meditative reading, and in prayerful recreations such as sitting in the garden, taking a walk in the Lord's presence, admiring and enjoying the birds and flowers. But the two hours prescribed by Rule should, of course, be devoted to, what we have called, unoccupied prayer. Until we have got the measure of ourselves and learned from experience, it would be well to seek guidance as to how much extra time we give to it. We may be wiser to engage in some 'secular' occupation or reading. On the other hand, our adviser may counsel greater generosity in prayer. Each and all must bear in mind Teresa's simple charter: prayer is your business, such is the purpose of our life in Carmel. If this is engraved in our consciousness, we are not likely to be niggardly in giving extra time to prayer.

The silence, the solitude, the strict enclosure – all are intended to aid us to constant communing with Our Lord throughout our days and nights. Ours is a *life* of *prayer* and we must make sure that it is. Unless it is our preoccupation, our deepest concern, it cannot be said that we are faithful Carmelites. It demands effort and patient practise to acquire the habit as well as the ascetical practices we were taught when we entered but easily forget as the years go by: custody of the eyes, mortification of our curiosity, care for deportment and so forth. Controlling our physical movements goes a long way to gaining inner control. We owe it, not only to ourselves but to our sisters, to cultivate a quiet, recollected exterior that does not intrude on others' attention and helps to establish and maintain an appropriate atmosphere in the monastery. Undue bustle and noise, lack of self-control, militate against it. Care for the development of our own prayer as well as thoughtfulness and concern for others, demands that we impose discipline on ourselves. If we really understand that prayer is our life, we will appreciate the necessity, not merely the advantage, of a strict silence and we will observe it with care, always reflecting before we speak and asking ourselves if what we intend to say is really necessary and if it is the right time and place in which to say it.

Silence enables us to live our lives from our personal centre, aware all the time of what we are doing and why we are doing it. It allows us to keep ourselves steadily directed towards the will of God, to recognise quickly when we have lost our directedness and equally speedily to reset the compass. In a loving community which has discarded many outworn customs and allows greater freedom on unimportant matters, there is a danger of becoming careless in the observance of silence, allowing ourselves little friendly exchanges and observations, imparting of a piece of news, cracking a joke, and the like. Everything of this kind, seemingly harmless, must be sacrificed. Without our being aware of it, it shapes a mentality, weakens us and the partner in the exchange. This easy-goingness can become an accepted standard within a community and becomes very difficult to correct.

The obligation to develop our human potential

Throughout this chapter there is an emphasis on 'passivity', a form of prayer that radically reduces our own

activity, allowing it a only minor role. To avoid any mis-
understanding we must recall that neither Teresa nor
John permit us wholly to abandon the use of our powers,
or to attempt to silence the mind completely. In speaking
of unoccupied prayer, a great deal is presupposed if the
passivity is not to be a barren waste of time. God does not
work miracles but purifies and transforms nature, what is
actually there. This simple fact means that we have a work
to do, a great work, that of developing our potential to the
full. Only insofar as potentiality is realised, can God give
himself to it. The more there is of us, the more is there for
God to transform and the more we are his glory. So a
mentality that fails to see the importance of maturation, of
intellectual and emotional development, thwarts, rather
than fosters contemplation. It is foolish to take our standard from the past when women's life was purely domestic
and there was little available with which to advance their
personal education. We can be sure God expects us to do
all we can to grow as persons, continually stretching and
deepening the mind, nourishing imagination and emotions, largely through a wide range of reading. Not
infrequently we may find ourselves emotionally disturbed,
bewildered and 'threatened' in what is dearest to our heart
– our faith and trust in God. No matter. There can be no
human development without pain, sense of loss, struggle,
self-knowledge. Everything depends on our response. If
we are faithful in prayer and in our daily life, we have
nothing to fear, whatever our feelings. The modern world
of exploration and discovery in astrophysics, psychology,
sexual ethics, genetics, to name but a few areas, inevitably
provokes serious questionings. Contemplatives must not
evade these questionings but face them serenely, refusing
to shelter behind worn-out, naive platitudes. God is ever

greater: too great for human mind or heart to compass. Faith, insofar as it is genuine, cannot be undermined, but only purified and deepened through exposure to reality which is, after all, a manifestation of God. Nothing can be a threat to *God*; there can be no problem in regard to God but only to our finite notions of God and these need constant purification. God completely transcends the range of thought whence problems arise and we lose nothing by the apparent loss or obscuration of the God we thought we knew. We are asked to live in the Mystery, 'shrouded in its own absence of categories',[11] yet known through Jesus to be absolute Love.

Members of a community can help to educate one another by a studied or unstudied sharing of their enthusiasm and knowledge at the time of recreation, as experience shows. The horarium, enclosure and community resources impose their own limitations and asceticism but, within these limits, the prioress in dialogue with her community should willingly provide what is necessary for developing culture. This provision will include creative activities such as painting, carving, embroidery, music and whatever accords with sisters' aptitudes.

Recollection throughout the day

I do not mean that it is not a favour from the Lord, if any of us is able to be continually meditating upon His works; and it is good for us to try to do this. But it must be realised that not everyone has by nature an imagination capable of meditating, whereas all souls are capable of love . . . the soul is not thought, nor is the will controlled by thought – it would be a great misfortune if it were. The soul's profit, then, consists not in thinking much but in loving much.[12]

To love is to choose, and this, in practice, means setting our hearts firmly on seeking and doing the will of God hour by hour. This constant directedness needs the support of the mind and so we choose to use our mind to supply strong motivation in order to keep the compass pointing steadily, and to reset it when it has wavered. To love God all the time does not mean thinking 'God-thoughts' all the time, and sending up a continuous spiral of pious ejaculations (though true love will think often of Our Lord and express its love interiorly), but it does mean choosing God all the time. Asceticism of the mind and imagination is essential. To allow thoughts to wander unchecked in areas that do not lead to greater love and fidelity is, itself, a serious infidelity and will result in lack of directedness. The mind must be trained to think good thoughts. A well-stocked, educated mind is a great asset, uplifting the personality above inner broodings tainted with self-pity and other selfish traits. In an earlier chapter allusion was made to the ever present danger in the enclosed life of indulging in undue reflections on the character and behaviour of our sisters, an evil which John of the Cross strenuously opposes in the Precautions.[13] He is uncompromising: if we allow ourselves distractions such as these we will never be contemplatives and not even good religious.

Finally, what better counsel can we find to help us understand the meaning of 'constant recollection', than the words of Paul:

> Whatever is true, whatever is honourable, whatever is just, whatever is pure, whatever is gracious, if there is any excellence, if there is anything worthy of praise, think about these things.[14]

CHAPTER ELEVEN

Asceticism

They will live in the strictest enclosure, never going out, and seeing no one without having veils over their faces, and the foundation of their lives will be prayer and mortification.[1]

This is how St Teresa describes the way of life she is planning for her reformed convent. Her formulation, 'the foundation of their lives will be prayer and mortification', has frequently been echoed by Church authorities in recent times. The canonical contemplative life in general, according to the mind of the Church, is a life of prayer and penance. We understand, to some extent at any rate, what is meant by a life of prayer, but can the same be said about a life of penance? What are we to think of penance? It is important to have clear ideas on the subject if we are to live authentically our ecclesial vocation of prayer and penance.

Until very recent times, penance was always associated, if not identified, with physical austerity and self-inflicted pain or deprivation. Religious history and a study of the schools of spiritualities, confirm the almost universal assumption that such austerities were indispensable on the path to holiness. Hagiographers delighted in recounting the amazing and often highly imaginative devices with which their spiritual heroes waged war on the poor body. Allowing for flights of fantasy and gross exaggerations in the recounting of such exploits, it would seem that, generally speaking, the spiritual value of hard physical austerity and self-inflicted pain was taken for granted. Teresa and John, children of their times as they were, shared this assumption. Teresa, it must be said, admired excess in persons she revered: Peter of Alcantara, for instance, and Catalina de Cordova, but, in practice, her common sense prevailed. In their direction of others, both Teresa and John were unfashionably moderate. This moderation is evident in Teresa's *Constitutions*, provided that we bear in mind the spiritual culture of sixteenth-century Spain.

The centuries-old attitude of harsh bodily chastisement arose from a dualism wholly unbiblical, in which matter – the body – was seen as the potential enemy of the spirit, imprisoning it and weighing it down. So the ascetic despised and feared it and sought to weaken its vital forces, hoping in this way to liberate the spirit. Even when undertaken by people inspired by love, as was often the case, we must question whether they were not falling back into ways of thinking that do not belong to the advent of the 'new' in Jesus. The deeply-rooted desire to do something for God, to have the satisfaction of feeling that we suffer for him and in this way prove – to ourselves – that we do love him, must humbly yield to becoming a child who, of course, has nothing to give but can only receive. The truly Christian attitude gladly allows God to be God, the giver, and descends from the throne, of, oh, so subtle a desire, to be 'as God' so as to meet God on some sort of equal base. The only way that we can give to him is by allowing him full control: to give to us, to work in us and through us. The initiative must always be his. We must give only what God asks us to give, not what we want to give; our attention precisely on watching for what is asked. Intent on doing things for God we fail to see what he is asking here and now and so miss many opportunities of 'returning love for love'.

Our thinking today has undergone a vast change. We have returned to scripture and to our one Master, Christ. It is to him alone that we look for a true understanding of ourselves, of our nature and of how we must live as the beloved of the Father. The Christian people continues to grow in a deep appreciation and reverence for the material creation and for the human body. We are struggling to free ourselves from inherited suspicion and contempt for our bodies and their functions and needs, rejecting the negative attitude to sexuality which for centuries has dogged the Christian Church. The last forty years have witnessed radical changes in Church discipline. Pius XII abolished the age-long Lenten fast, restricting Church fasts to two days in the year, Ash Wednesday and Good Friday. The eucharistic fast, from midnight to the time of communion, was modified to one hour only, and the Friday abstinence abolished. In no way was this gentler discipline absolving the faithful from the asceticism and self-denial inseparable from true discipleship. Moreover, reverence for creation imposes its own restraints with a vigorous rejection of possessiveness and greed.

When we turn to Jesus who reveals the way God wants us to live, there is nothing whatever to suggest that self-inflicted hardship and pain are pleasing to his Father. The Father whom Jesus reveals hates useless suffering. Jesus never asked his followers to do something hard for its own sake. On the contrary, in his Father's name, he showed himself the enemy of pain, putting an end to it whenever he could, be it hunger, bodily sickness or mental anguish and grief. What is more, the vision of the Father that he revealed, implicitly did away with the notion that he could be placated, appeased by our doing hard things and punishing ourselves, atoning for our sins by fasting and the like. The friends of the bridegroom do not fast when the bridegroom is with them. Jesus is always with us and the Father always turned to us in love. There is no need whatever to 'bring him round' by offering him hard and hurtful things. It is we who have to be 'brought round', converted, (the biblical meaning of penance), turned right round to stand full-face to him. Our hearts must be broken with loving sorrow, not our bodies buffeted and bruised. This is fasting indeed.

Looking at St Teresa's *Constitutions* and the companion *The Way of Perfection*, we clearly discern that, in her mind, physical asceticism had a two-fold purpose or function. She shared the current understanding of its apostolic fruitfulness. In prescribing the discipline – universally employed for personal, self-inflicted mortification – she is explicit as to its intention. It is 'for the increase of faith, for benefactors, for souls in purgatory, for captives and for those in mortal sin.'[2] She is less explicit in *The Way of Perfection*, grieving over the lamentable state of the Church:

> If your prayers and desires and disciplines and fasts are not performed for the intentions of which I have spoken, reflect that you are not carrying out the work for which God has brought you here.[3]

We are, understandably, uncomfortable with this language

and are justified in rejecting it but, as we see with Teresa herself, the idea it expresses easily merges into an understanding of austerity, that we readily embrace.

Jesus asks us to deny ourselves, take up our cross and follow him and this involves the denial of self-seeking in all its forms so as to be set free to love God and our neighbour, 'sharing his suffering so as to share his glory'. The asceticism which characterises Teresian legislation is part of this cross. Prayer and self-indulgence do not go together and prayer is synonymous with the surrender of self. The austerity of our life-style is an expression of our longing for God, of a desire for a radical and continual 'conversion' so as to belong to God alone, devoting ourselves – body, heart and mind – to him. This means that our natural instincts, drives, energies – all must be harnessed and directed to God so that, in very truth, 'whether we eat or drink, whatever we do, all is done for the glory of God'.

Teresa herself – as she expressly says – deprecates 'excessive penance, which, if practised indiscreetly, may injure the health'.[4] Rather, she puts the weight on the interior virtues of humility, detachment from self, love of neighbour, and these of course, are the great virtues of the Gospel. However, a balanced physical austerity is indispensable for our single-minded aim of total prayer. Teresa has no doubt about it. 'The first thing, then, that we have to do, and that at once, is to rid ourselves of love for this body of ours.'[5] The context makes quite clear what she means by this radical statement. Energetically she insists that her nuns are not to be 'softies', not fussy about their health, but coping maturely with small indispositions.

Do not think of complaining about the weaknesses and minor ailments from which women suffer . . . They come and go; and unless

117

you get rid of the habit of talking about them and complaining of everything (except to God) you will never come to the end of them.[6]

She is well aware that danger lurks in an enclosed life in which there is little diversion and little comfort. Minor ailments, mood changes, impinge far more keenly on the consciousness. This is something that must be faced early in formation and sisters helped to understand what is happening and embrace their difficult times with unselfish love. It is salutary to remember the lot of millions of women the world over and compare it with our own. A robustness of spirit is called for – a human determination prompted and sustained by grace, to forget oneself at those times when it is easy to fall into self-pity and self-preoccupation.

St Teresa's seemingly uncompromising attitude of 'toughness' regarding the body and the imperative that the individual forgets herself, must be set alongside her concern for the sick. Moreover, she takes it for granted that, in her monasteries,

> . . . where there is prayer and charity among you, and your numbers are so small that you will be aware of each others' needs, there will never be any lack of care in your being looked after.[7]

The individual sister herself must assume a proper responsibility for her health. After all, we belong to the community; our bodily health is not ours to squander. Teresa obliges the sisters to tell the prioress and the novices their mistress whatever genuine difficulty they have with the common provisions, even though their need for exceptions is not great. But always anxious lest we chip away at the sacrificial element which must be present

in our life, she enjoins on us to pray over the matter first
for

> ... our human nature often asks for more than what it needs, and
> sometimes the devil helps so as to cause fear about the practice of
> penance and fasting.[8]

Our vows of poverty and obedience must incline us to
accept the common life even at cost, rather than seek
exemptions. Here is an inbuilt austerity, not of our choosing, which, in a caring community with a caring superior,
can be shirked in all sorts of ways. Such instances are
asking to retire early because one is feeling tired, or heart-
sick and emotionally upset, and seeking escape in sleep.
To do so is to miss the opportunity for growth in self-
knowledge and self-surrender. We may seek the little
comforts of snacks in between meals; may ask for a change
of occupation when our present one is irksome or someone we work with difficult; we may demand more or less
air or heat in the common places, and all in the name of
health. Again, we can exploit one aspect of the life-style –
our work, for instance – to avoid another we find difficult.
As Teresa points out ironically, few superiors are going to
refuse our requests when health is involved and the fact
that they concede does not absolve us from responsibility.

> The sick should be cared for with fullness of love, concern for their
> comfort, and compassion in accordance with the poverty we prac-
> tice.[9]

We learn from many sources of St Teresa's great compassion for the sick. The first thing she did on arriving at one
of her monasteries, after she had spent a few minutes in
the chapel, was to visit the sick. Her letters too testify to

her concern for her daughters' health. In her *Constitutions* she goes so far as to say that

> . . . the Mother Prioress should be very careful that the healthy nuns be deprived of something necessary rather than that anything be wanting to the sick.[10]

Today, in our culture, this necessity is unlikely to be food or medication but the needs of the sick may make big demands on our time, energy and sleep. At the same time, she exhorts the sick to use their illness to grow in love, to be patient and thoughtful for others, trying to cause as little trouble as possible. Should they feel the pinch of poverty, lacking what the well-to-do might have, they must not complain for, on entering religious life, they embraced the way of poverty. To be poor in reality is to lack necessities in time of greatest need.

Teresa's legislation is singularly detailed regarding organised austerity: she legislates for the house, furniture, bedding, clothing, food. Encasing all is the structure of the Rule with its round of prayer and work, which in itself is an asceticism. This has been touched on already but it will not come amiss to draw attention once more to some specific asceticisms built into the life-style. Only a wholehearted generosity will ensure that they fulfil their purpose. Such are constant attendance in choir and the effort to give of our best; the diligent execution of whatever work is assigned to us; the restrictions, deprivations and inconveniences attendant on enclosure; the self-denial involved in living a community life according to the mind of Jesus; the emotional and mental 'fasting' inherent in a sincere living of the vows and a life of pure faith; unswerving fidelity to two hours of personal prayer each day.

Moreover, this moderate but all-pervading asceticism must be embraced whatever our emotional state and this, of course, demands an interior asceticism of the emotions. Its sole purpose is to set us free from ourselves so as to be wholly open to receive God's love. *This* is *our* apostolate; *this* is the way in which our prayers, our desires, our penances, our fasts are of benefit to others. The more a person is possessed by God, living Jesus' life, the more she herself transmits life. It is not our vocation to preach the word, to engage in any outward apostolate – that vocation belongs to others, but the opening of hearts to the word, its fruiting, is ultimately and solely the work of the Spirit. 'God alone gives the increase.' Holiness is the channel for the transmission of the Spirit.

The house and grounds

We must keep in mind that St Teresa's Reform was a reaction to the way of life in her former community and in many monasteries of her acquaintance. This is important for a balanced assessment of her legislation. The house, she ordains, 'must be small and the rooms humble: something that fulfils rather than exceeds the need'.[11] It should be well built but never adorned with anything finely wrought and the wood should be rough. Teresa's book *Foundations* as well as her letters give a lively account of her own procedures when planning a foundation. She commissioned her friends to look for a house of adequate size – or with the possibility of expansion – in a suitable neighbourhood. Occasionally, she was given a house, which, even though not ideal, she accepted but did not hesitate to exchange it for a better one later on. Unless a community is given an adequate sum of money to build the ideal from the ground, Teresa's procedure is the only feasible one. She herself enjoyed one opportunity to build from the ground according to her own plans, and so we have a model of her ideal.

'Large', 'small', are relative terms. Everything depends on the context. In the case of enclosed nuns, the 'small' house must provide the space for possibly over twenty nuns, for their liturgical worship, recreation, work, meals in common, and for an extensive library. Moreover, each sister is to have a separate cell in which she not merely sleeps but spends time praying, reading, working. Further, remunerative work is an inalienable part of our Rule and this demands suitable premises. Recognising as we must, that the needs of women today differ from those of earlier times, there must be rooms for craft work, for painting perhaps, for weaving – whatever. To provide for all this is wholly consonant with the foundress' stipulation that we attend to what is necessary, not to what is super-fluous.

With the exception of the church, the house should not be adorned; the woodwork must be rough. Does this mean a cult of drabness and ugliness? Nothing in Teresa's writings or of what is told of her allows us to think so. She was delighted when she managed to purchase a fine house – the very best in the neighbourhood! We cannot imagine her setting out to deface it. However, whatever she felt of the aesthetic and emotional needs of her nuns, we need not scruple today to make our house aesthetically pleasing, worthy of a house of God, for that is what it is. The human heart is not uplifted by drabness, by dark, dingy rooms. There are ways of ensuring a simple, even austere beauty that reflects our profession of poverty, simple lifestyle and desert orientation, with its yearning for God alone. Often, it will mean making the very best of what we have inherited and are not in a position to reverse. As to the added adornment of curtains, carpets and cushions, these, of course, are out of the question. Teresa is emphatic on the matter. Such things do not belong to religious observance.[12] We know from the *Foundations* and from her letters, how much Teresa valued fine views, and she surrounded her monasteries with ample grounds, enough for the building of hermitages, where the nuns could enjoy periods of greater solitude. It is clear from her letters that the nuns cultivated gardens. Today, it is essential that enclosed women have grounds wholly adequate for physical and psychological health. Experience reveals that, generally speaking, environment affects the personality. Space, beauty, light, are more likely to foster breadth of mind and a sense of beauty, as well as help to cheerfulness of spirit than cramped, dingy living conditions. A deleterious consequence of a small enclosure is that it can make excursions seem reasonable and, indeed, perhaps necessary to preserve physical and psychic health. However, this is an undesirable state of affairs and must not be taken as a wholly acceptable interpretation of Carmelite life today.

Clothing and bedding

As we would expect, St Teresa wished her nuns to identify with the poorer classes in the way they lived. Their clothing – habit and underwear, as well as bedding – was to be of the cheap coarse wool in use among the ordinary people. The woollen industry flourished in Spain during Teresa's lifetime and was, in fact, the staple of the economy of Castile. Silk, fine wool and linen were available for the wealthy, but the ordinary people used the same coarse homespun that Teresa gave to her nuns. In doing so, she was not devising a night-and-day hairshirt, but giving practical expression to the vow of poverty, and to detachment from everything 'worldly'. The same must be said for the straw palliasse, sufficient, in her experience, even for the aged and infirm; not a nocturnal penance but an adoption of the usage of the lower classes. Our loyalty to her spirit leads us to use the common materials of our day. Woollen fabrics are expensive whereas hard wearing, long-lasting synthetics relatively cheap. What is more, they are labour-saving and easily washed. A modern standard of hygiene is imperative. Some of us can look back to our young days, to when woollen sheets and pillow cases were changed only once a year. Considering the Amazonian strength needed to heave sopping-wet thick woollen or serge sheets in and out of tubs, scrub them clean and wring them out, having to rely on fine weather to dry them, it is no wonder. As for habits, they were rarely washed, if at all. Nor does fidelity demand that we make our own mattresses of hessian and straw – still less, wear stockings of the same hessian!

Teresa prescribes exactly how the habit must be made and in doing so is radically rejecting the all-too-common practice of nuns, who, while still claiming to wear a habit, ensured it being of the finest material, with graceful trailing skirt and wide sleeves. The habit of the discalced nun was, on the contrary, to be as sparse as possible; the same length back and front and reaching to the ankles. The toques were to be made of coarse linen and without pleats.[13] We have no reason for assuming that this feminine woman intended to deny a woman's innocent instinct to dress becomingly and to oblige her nuns to look 'frumps'. The fact that they were rarely seen save by their own companions is irrelevant. A woman's self-respect is involved. There is a distinction, and a big one, to be made between that simple need and a preoccupation with appearance that takes time and attention. This is alien to the vocation. But just as we advocate rejecting an ethos of drabness in our houses, so with our personal appearance. Wearing a uniform habit ensures that we do not have to spend time wondering what to wear and whether this or that suits us. We have the assurance that our habit is clean, neat, dignified and becoming, as befits a woman consecrated to God. More importantly, it is a constant reminder to us of what we are and what our profession. Ordinarily, the way we dress is a form of self-expression; an attempt to express outwardly who we think we are. For us, the habit tells us all we need to know and can know: we are Carmelites, dedicated to God, who alone knows who and what we are and is bringing us to our full personhood.

Eating and drinking

The legislation on fasting must be reinterpreted. St Teresa was following the universal monastic custom of observing a fast from the feast of the Exaltation of the Holy Cross until Easter. We are right in recognising here something deriving from a culture, as well as from a theology that we have re-thought. Maybe it was a matter of making a virtue of necessity. In the northern hemisphere from late autumn to late spring, the population existed on food stored from the previous harvest; on salted meat, and whatever animals or birds could be hunted down. The monks might have a well-stocked fish-pond but the pond could freeze and the fish die. Food shortage was a perpetual hazard until the blessed growing season returned once more.

The very word 'fast' is, or was, ambiguous. In Church usage it meant one full meal a day, allowing for a small collation in the evening and in the morning. One could rightly ask whether that is not the norm by choice, for many people today. If so, 'fasting' in the above sense is meaningless.

Surely we are more in keeping with the spirit of Jesus if we simply accept our necessary food with gratitude, taking responsibility for keeping ourselves as healthy and as strong as possible, in order to serve him in the community. However, to follow Jesus as perfectly as possible we must be free and this calls for asceticism. We may not allow our natural instincts to dominate us in any way but must harness them to the service of love. So, moderation is needed, neither over-eating nor under-eating. For us who live in community, our asceticism lies largely in accepting contentedly and gratefully the common fare, whether it is to our taste or not. Very properly, St Teresa forbids her sisters to make any comment as to whether the food is well or badly prepared.[14] Such complaints cut clean across our profession of a life of poverty, of dependence on God's loving providence. We do not eat or drink (save water) between meals and choice dishes and delicacies are reserved for special celebrations.

The prioress and those responsible for the sisters' diet have a serious obligation to take advantage of modern dietetics and cookery. They must be studied to ensure that the community is provided with a nourishing and well balanced daily diet. If the sisters know that this is the case, they can lay aside preoccupation and anxiety, and accept trustfully what is provided. A well cooked, well balanced and nicely served daily fare affects a community's physical, emotional, and therefore spiritual well-being far more than was recognised – if it was recognised at all. Depression, sluggishness, obesity, the tendency to need more sleep – are some of the possible effects of an unsuitable diet. Women entering the monastery today are likely to be well aware of this. We are imposing an unnecessary burden on them, a 'penance' God could not want, if, through ignorance and mistaken ideas of 'mortification', we oblige them, because they have no other source of sustenance, to eat what they know is unhealthy.

The practice of poverty

St Teresa's implementation in daily life of the vow of poverty, was extremely radical and, once again, we do well to remember that she was reacting to life in the Monastery of the Incarnation at Avila. Her rigorism in this matter was practiced well into and beyond the mid-twentieth century. Every piece of clothing, including underwear, was kept in the appropriate office and dispensed when needed or at the proper time and season. Sizes apart, there was uniformity in cut and material and the day was fixed for the change from winter to summer underwear. Anything not routinely delivered had to be asked for and this included the most intimate of toilet needs. No one had a chest or cupboard in her cell for her personal effects. The cells contained only the basics: a bed, a stool, a table if there were no window-ledge on which to write, a small shelf for a lamp and water jug, and one for a few books. Some sort of container for the materials needed for a modest hobby was allowed. Teresa's stress was on the common life: no personal possessions, everything in common.

> In no way should the Sisters have any particular possessions, nor should such permissions be granted; nothing in the way of food or clothing; nor should they have any coffer or small chest, or box, or cupboards . . . everything must be held in common.[15]

Needless to say, modern life has made change imperative and some personal 'possessions' are inevitable: for example, underclothes are personal and kept by the individual. Moreover, all normal needs, be they sheets, towels, remedies for minor ailments, notepaper, envelopes, toilet requisites, and so on, should be available without recourse to the officers, still less to the prioress. This not only saves time but also unnecessary intercourse.

Nevertheless, this freedom calls for watchfulness and honesty with ourselves. Carelessness, extravagance, taking things for granted, behaving as people do who can put their hands in their pockets at any time – we can only avoid these and other pitfalls by *wanting* to understand the spirit of Carmel and the radical gift of self it requires, and *determining* to fulfil its requirements. The removal in many areas, of the minute controls and uniformity of former days, acts as a sword that divides and reveals the thoughts of our hearts. It is good for us to know the price of things and to consider how we would act if we had to fend for ourselves on a low income. Having everything we need, never knowing want, there is always a danger of taking things for granted and forgetting the realities of life outside. We might well bear in mind the injunction of St John of the Cross to seek to have less rather than more.

Work

St Teresa, as we know, took up with enthusiasm the injunction of the Rule that the brethren should work. In common with countless housewives all over Castile, the sisters joined the wool trade and could always be sure of a market for their work. Industriousness characterised the Teresian monasteries, for the sisters were trained not to waste a moment of the time allotted to work and to have their distaffs with them at recreation and even when seeing visitors in the parlour. Teresa herself set the example. Everyone, including the prioress, was to share in the ordinary domestic chores of the house. Here was a context for selfless giving, a genuine asceticism.

Life for us is vastly more complex than it was for those early Carmelites and suitable work is not readily available. Inevitably, modern economics have, so to speak, changed the face of Carmel – the face, not the soul, not the inner spirit. Telephones, typewriters, computers, fax machines and the like, have become a normal part of a monastery's equipment. The acquisition of each one of these inventions needs careful reflection and an effort to see its implications for our way of life. That a thing is in common use today, does not mean that it is right for us to introduce it into the monastery. The discernment to see which commodities of modern life have a proper place in our life and which have not, once again depends on our grasp of the charism and love for it. As we all know, today's necessity was yesterday's luxury. Where do we draw the line? These are not easy decisions to make.

Though we are spared the physical hardships of earlier times, maybe we have pressures that our sisters of those days could not know and these provide us with asceticism. True, we all find pleasure and satisfaction in work, but also plenty of frustration, fatigue and maybe natural boredom. The modern woman will take less easily than a woman of past centuries to the often dull, monotonous work of Carmel, but the more we see our work as a service of love and undertake it cheerfully, the less notice we will take of those natural reactions.

It is essential to understand that hard work is a vital element in the charism. In taking on the Rule of Carmel we take on a burden of work. Hard work is ordained precisely towards contemplation. It is not an unfortunate necessity. There is always a danger of associating contemplative life with an existence of leisure, with having a lot of time for oneself to reflect, to pray and be continually aware of God's presence. Of course we need time and space to reflect, and time to devote exclusively to prayer, but equally, we need the discipline of hard work and the opportunity it provides for unselfing. It imposes a healthy discipline on the mind and emotions and is an effective instrument of purification. Work roots us in the reality of Jesus, in our own humanity and in solidarity with our fellow human beings.

If our work is to fulfil its sanctifying purpose we need to examine and, when needed, correct our attitudes. We can work egotistically. We can, for instance, give overmuch time and attention to an aspect of it that will be seen and appreciated, or that we ourselves enjoy, striving there for 'perfection', to the neglect of other things. Rather, we must act with detachment, arranging things and allotting the appropriate amount of time to each task, according to objective norms, not according to our own preferences. Proper detachment, coupled with a serious approach to our work, will prompt us to make good arrangements and a proportioning of time that enables a great deal to be accomplished in the hours appointed. Stress may, of course, indicate that we have too much work, but first, let us examine our attitude in the light of the above. As often as not, stress indicates a lack of detachment. It may be that we are too anxious to please, to 'succeed' and are afraid of appearing inadequate. Work time is for work; in its own way as sacred as prayer time, and may not, without permission, be used for anything else. Nor may we work in a leisurely fashion and assume that, once we have completed our quota, the rest of the time is ours. If we find that we have not been assigned sufficient tasks to fill the appointed hours, we should let it be known, and maybe we can relieve others who, perhaps, have too many. Let us not forget that our Rule obliges us to earn money, whether we need the money ourselves or not. What we do not need is to be given alms. Our time, our working capacity, belong to God and others.

The daily, unobtrusive, unselfconscious asceticism that the faithful living of the Rule of Carmel demands, is by far the most effective. It is not likely to afford self-satisfaction but it is what God asks of us, and that is what is important. To take on an extra, a 'penance', in order to give God something that costs, is, however subtly, presuming to accord the 'I' some control over God, whereas the 'I' has to be surrendered: God must be allowed all the initiative and full control. Only in this way will each of us become the person, the self God created her to be. If a suffering should fall to us, from which there is no escape, then we shall know that this is what Divine Love is asking us to bear in love, and this we shall do in his strength, not in our own. 'Not to us, Lord, not to us, but to your Name give the glory.'[16]

CHAPTER TWELVE

Formation

The first step in the long process of formation is the selection of candidates. No one can pretend that this is easy, whether in reference to the initial reception or of progressive integration into the community. Still, we must try to say something on the subject.

Selection

It goes without saying that we cannot hope to educate a woman for the Carmelite life unless she is suitable material. Before suggesting what qualities to look for, we need to remind ourselves of an underlying principle. It is this: each one of us, be we superiors or members of the chapter, have the duty to protect the authentic charism of Carmel at whatever cost to ourselves. We may not allow unsuitable candidates to reach profession. We can aptly apply to ourselves the deep concern of our foundress for the difficulties the Church was experiencing in her day, and her determination that her Carmels should be unequivocally committed to the welfare of the Church, disregarding themselves and their selfish concerns.

Surely today it is vital that the Carmelite way of life

should be lived with great purity, but this is impossible where there is lack of vocation, lack of real understanding.

It causes me deadly pain to think there can be any house of ours in which things are worse than in the houses of the Calced in Andalusia. I have been unfortunate in the house of Malagon.[1]

This obligation must override our very natural and understandable desire to survive as a community, and to have much needed help in carrying the burden of work. Great abandonment and self-sacrifice are called for. Only if we face this honestly, search our hearts as best we can, so as to uncover our basic desire and motivation, and pray earnestly for singleness of purpose, may we hope to maintain objectivity in the process of discernment. Given singlemindedness which engages in a serious investigation of the life and character of the aspirant, then we confidently trust that the decision we reach is according to God's will. After all, we have only human ways in which to discover it and, at this preliminary stage, all we are doing is making an informed guess that this particular woman has the necessary qualities and possibly a call from God.

However, there may be asked of us a still more costly sacrifice. Unless our juridical autonomy is matched by autonomy of life which includes

. . . enough resources and personnel for a faithful Teresian Carmelite observance and formation and government, so as to give assurances for the vitality of the monastery, its development and its future needs . . .[2]

we may not receive a postulant, for the simple reason that

we cannot offer her an authentic Carmelite life. This is a matter of justice.

We might argue that a responsible adult needs no protection from us and if she chooses to enter our particular monastery, she should be allowed to do so. But we know well enough that certain temperaments, caught up in religious fervour, are liable to be susceptible to the rhetoric of sacrifice. To take advantage of this with persuasive spiritual eloquence, is surely a serious wrong. We can cause immense damage, spiritual and emotional, for which, sadly, there is ample testimony.

That painful nettle grasped, and presuming we are a viable, autonomous community, what should we look for in aspirants? To begin with, there has to be a call from God and the only evidence that this might be so comes from the person herself. It is she who has expressed desire and is acting upon that desire: she gets in touch, visits and continues with the process of investigation according to the community's norms. There are practical signs that will tell us immediately that, whatever the subjective desire or intuition, this enquirer is not called to Carmel. If God gives the vocation to a particular way of life, it must be a practical possibility, and so we can rule out immediately someone who, for instance, has other commitments, suffers from a chronic illness or has a recognised mental disorder. Then, even when a vocation remains a possibility, it will take years before the candidate or ourselves can affirm it with certitude.

We all know that it is the personality of the aspirant which challenges our perspicacity. St Teresa, in her formal writings and letters, has much to say. Clearly she was made painfully aware, after some years had passed and problems had arisen, that many mistakes had been made; mistakes for which, once the subject was solemnly professed, there was no remedy, and the community was from then on, burdened with a troublemaker perhaps, or a mere 'passenger', and maybe a 'weepy wailly' demanding everyone's attention and sympathy.

> As there are very few of us, such unrest is caused when one of our number proves unsuited to the Order that even a person with not much conscience would feel scrupulous about taking her . . . [3]

Teresa gives us, in the *Foundations*(ch7) as well as in her correspondence, some idea of the havoc 'non-vocations' could cause, especially those afflicted with 'melancholy'. This seems to be a blanket term for various aspects of neurosis. It is not surprising therefore, that besides good health, the foundress demands intelligence and good judgment.[4] A person of genuine intelligence and balanced mind is more likely to understand herself and others and live in reality. Teresa wanted women of character and was not interested in an aspirant who was 'no more than a very nice girl'.[5]

To a friar she writes, somewhat provocatively, since he is pressing her to oblige a community to accept the 'unsuited' person referred to above:

> I was amused at Your Reverence's remark that you could sum her up immediately if once you saw her. We women cannot be summed up as easily as that . . . If you want us to serve you in these houses of ours, my Father, send us women of ability and you will see that we shall not be the least worried about their dowries.[6]

If an aspirant is to have a comprehensive understanding of our life, and respond to the values that are put before her, she must be intelligent and well educated.

On no account take postulants who are not sensible people, for it is
against our constitutions to do so, and the harm is incurable.[7]

True, a profound grasp of the charism is a spiritual gift
but the soil for it is natural intelligence. A postulant must
be able to read well: theology, scripture, spiritual classics
and books of a general nature that continually advance her
culture and human development. In a life of enclosure, of
silence and solitude, there can be no reliance on others to
provide stimulus, each must find it for herself. Hence, the
necessity of education and intelligence. However, a person
may have academic brilliance and a dazzling ability to
articulate the charism and yet lack what Teresa calls 'good
judgment' and we 'common sense', the ready ability to
apply ideas and principles into the workaday world of
Carmelite living. It cannot be taught, but if a person has
enough spirituality and the humility to accept that she
lacks this faculty, whether she comes to realise it herself
through lived experience, or takes it on the word of
another, and readily submits to guidance, all can be well.
Such humility is rare. Not infrequently, 'clever' people
who lack judgment seem singularly devoid of humility
and are inclined to believe that they are the ones who have
got it right and and everyone else is woefully benighted.
It is not difficult to detect deep emotional problems lying
behind their self-righteous obstinacy. No matter how
rational and objective the arguments seem – and many are
impressed – they are, in fact, emotional, emerging from
the sticky morass of unrecognised fears of inadequacy and
the like. Such clever, persuasive, but emotionally unbal-
anced people are a danger. The trouble is that the
emotional sickness is not obvious, for these people are well
behaved, 'model religious', and it may take a long time for

it to be generally recognised and then only when damage is done. Other serious emotional disturbances are more obvious and of course, we do not consider applicants in whom they are manifest.

Undoubtedly, we will sigh for the ideal candidates, those with every natural quality: a finely balanced mind, rich and robust emotional life, a sense of humour, an ease in relationships, creativity, 'sparkle'. If such come they are a boon to a community, provided, of course, that they have a true vocation. But the ideal aside, if a community is to be healthy and strong, then the largest proportion of its members must be well balanced and intelligent. Difficulties in discernment arise when we perceive that an aspirant has some emotional difficulties but, not, seemingly, of a serious nature. Do we perforce reject her or do we allow her to try? After all, none of us, or very few, have not suffered from some emotional disorder and found life in Carmel to be therapeutic. There is no clear answer, no generalisation and the following is merely an airing of possibilities.

We have the safeguard of a long probation but the longer a sister stays, becoming more and more part of the family, even though her psychological weaknesses are apparent to all, unless her behaviour is outrageous, there is sure to be a strong emotional reaction from some members of the community to her dismissal. Affection, compassion, the desire to be kind and loving, prevent an objective judgment. Then too, the longer the stay in Carmel, the harder it is for the sister to return to secular life. These factors suggests that it is better to act sooner, even at the risk of sending someone away who, given time, *might* have won through. A preliminary, lengthy live-in can be revealing and yet there is a radical difference between a live-in, no matter how exposed to the realities of Carmelite life, and the postulancy, when the door closes behind the person and she is no longer a visitor, a looker-on, but has made an initial decision for Carmel, and is committed now to the whole ascesis of living in community, under authority. Taking a more positive view of the issues we face, have we not proof among some of us, now solidly and happily rooted in Carmel, that emotional disorders and immaturities can be healed by a generous embracing of the whole ascesis of the life and surrender to God in prayer? A lot depends on the gravity of the disorder and that may not be assessable for some time.

Neurosis (the term is used here to cover any sort of psychological disorder) is essentially self-centred. That is the core of the ailment – an intense absorbing need to protect the frightened, wounded self against the bruising and buffeting of life, and hence the desire to manipulate circumstances, to gain and maintain control to ensure its protection. Of course, to some extent, we all experience this urge and much of our asceticism revolves around the denial of it, a turning constantly from self to God and others. Here we are considering those in whom this tendency is extreme. In treating of the affliction of 'melancholia' Teresa insists – and experience over and over proves her right – that, no matter how much we understand the cause of a sister's neurosis and rightly feel compassion, we must demand of her the same obedience, good behaviour, and faithful observance as of all. She must realise that no concessions will be made on account of her painful condition. When talking with her in private we can assure her that we understand and sympathise but, believing in her as we do, we are siding with her better, maturer self, and for that reason must be uncompromising. If she wants to live in Carmel then she must accept this discipline.

As Teresa herself found, if a person is intelligent, accepts that she is neurotic and appreciates the respect and love which will not 'coddle' her nor allow her to have her own way, all can be very well indeed. Even an acute neurosis can be dismembered and neutralised. The sister's inner wounds may still bleed, at least from time to time, and she may have to struggle to the end of her days with trying aspects of her temperament, but she is basically free, no longer governed by inner compulsions, and able to love. This is all we ask for.

Obviously, this 'neurosis' or disorder belongs in the more serious category and yet, perhaps, does not reveal itself until some years have passed. A neurosis is not incompatible with genuine spirituality. Nevertheless, while it exists, because of the basic ego-concentration, the spirituality is crippled. Genuine liberation means hard work and the brave endurance of pain for the sister herself, but also it makes heavy demands on those directly concerned with her. It may be years before the goal is reached. A community, and in particular the prioress and those directly responsible for selection and formation, must be realistic. Is the community strong enough to 'carry' such a person? Strong enough to support a 'failure'? Are the formation personnel capable of training such a one? It is always better to err on the side of dismissal rather than burden a community with a neurotic sister and entrap her in a way of life to which she is unsuited and which, later on, she cannot abandon without a trauma.

If, during the time of probation up to first vows, it becomes clear that the disorders are too grave to be healed by ordinary means and there is need of professional help, dismissal seems the wise course. Formation for Carmel and the process of psychotherapy are incompatible. A novice learning to be a contemplative and at the same time undergoing psychotherapy, will be totally confused and her relationship with her superiors impaired. All her energy and attention has to go into the process of psychotherapy if it is to be effective and she will have none left for what Carmel is teaching her.

As for ourselves, we need to be very clear in our own minds that we are not called to dabble in the art of psychotherapy or even of 'counselling'. Undoubtedly, it is right for us to acquire a sound knowledge of the principles involved and study to understand those in our care. Inevitably and rightly, we 'counsel' as any wise women do, but equally we direct, correct and make demands. Our area is the religious and spiritual life. We can only work successfully when our novice is a sufficiently integrated and mature person and then our formation should advance her personal growth.

If a postulant or novice constantly hankers for little concessions, finds community life stressful and blames members of the community for this and, likewise, if this work or that work is stressful, whereas another is relaxing, and if she does not submit wholeheartedly to authority, taking direction and correction seriously, then we rightly conclude that this pattern of evasion reveals that the candidate is not suited to the religious life. We may not concede and cushion her from difficult aspects of the life. Its realities must be faced, accepted generously or she must leave. We may not tailor the observance to her measure.

The trouble is that such individuals interpret the firm

approach as lack of understanding and are quick to detect where, in the community, sympathy is to be found. As manipulation has by now become a highly developed art, even though unconscious, they attract sympathy and support from one or more members of the community, who are not in a position to know the whole truth, and who, by temperament, incline always to the 'soft, kind, gentle' approach, not discerning that this may well be unkind, contrary to the sister's best interest and, of course, to that of the community. Any newcomer who, for whatever reason, becomes a divisive factor in a community, is suspect. But it is incumbent on the part of the chapter sisters to be completely loyal to the prioress and to the one who, with the consent of her council, she has appointed as novice mistress. Of course they may, and even must, voice their anxieties to them and even to the whole chapter, but it would be very wrong indeed, to communicate to a novice by any sign whatsoever, that they are 'on her side' versus those in authority. In this issue, the chapter sisters are bound by their vow to be steadfastly with the prioress, even though they may hold a different opinion.

It is likewise very wrong for a sister in community to make a friend and confidante of someone in formation, or to receive her confidences without the permission of the prioress. On the other hand, a newcomer who really understands the life, and seriously seeks to give herself to God, is not likely to indulge in this evasion and the fact that she does so itself raises doubts. However, every postulant must, in fairness, be given the time and opportunity to understand what Carmel asks of her, freely decide to accept all the exigencies of the life and reveal this in her conduct, or leave. For a sister of the community to collude with her evasions, no matter for what misguided kindness, is a betrayal of the newcomer. A really serious situation arises when the novice mistress herself gets emotionally involved, 'uses' a novice for the satisfaction of her need of love and friendship and so loses her objectivity. How much worse for the prioress herself to do so. The prioress can override the novice mistress when it comes to the point, but the reverse is not true. If it is the prioress who has lost her head to her heart, all the mistress can do, if her protests are ignored, is to make it clear to the chapter, in as discreet and respectful way as possible, that she holds a different opinion, and give the reasons why she thinks the novice should be dismissed. If the chapter votes along with the prioress then the responsibility is no longer hers. All she can do is to help the sister to see and correct her failings and improve. St Teresa saw the importance of the closest collaboration between the prioress and mistress, so that one interpretation of the charism is being transmitted, that the novices are not receiving double messages, and any attempt to play the one superior off against the other, is foiled. The two must trust one another. Teresa ensured this unity of direction by ruling that the prioress herself chose the one she wanted to hold the office. It is good for the prioress to have a hand in formation without in any way rescinding the novice mistress's overall direction and responsibility. She should get to know the novices and establish a real relationship with them. It may happen that she understands a particular novice better than the mistress and can give the helping hand that is needed. However, she has to see that a novice does not subtly evade the mistress because she thinks her inadequate or does not find her comforting and congenial, and watch too that she is not indulging an emotional attachment to herself. More will said of these emotional attachments. The matter is delicate and needs sensitive handling.

The novice mistress

The title is far from satisfactory but, as it is difficult to find an adequate substitute, we adhere to it. 'The novice mistress should be very prudent, prayerful and spiritual',[8] enjoins St Teresa. To be appointed to this office can mean a decisive grace of conversion, of more total commitment to God. But it will make heavy demands. The one chosen will be obliged, not only to study everything related to the charism which she is to transmit, but to search her own heart, look at the reality of her convictions, try to discern what is false, shallow, 'ungiven' and hold these out to God for healing, and this, not once, but over and over again. No one can do so much harm in this delicate office as a *poseur*, one who pretends to a spirituality and union with God which, in fact, she has not. It must be added that this happens unconsciously and is, alas, all too common among spiritual people. Anyone of us at any time can fall into this illusion, at least to some extent. Our only safeguard is the urgent and constant plea: 'Lord, that I may see!', and then being alert to this ever-present tendency in ourselves, and the resolve to exploit to the full the opportunities daily offered to us, to taste the bitter herb of self-knowledge. Unless we really want the truth, we fail to notice, brush off occasions, excuse ourselves, withdraw in thought and emotion from what disturbed us. Young as she was, St Thérèse clearly perceived the snare that lay in wait for her just as it did for others. Her loving but spiritually keen gaze detected the 'pretence' in those around her, even in those she loved most. It is the 'fervent' who are at risk, precisely those who care, who believe they want to belong wholly to God – but on their own terms:

> ... that is the difficulty ... for where are we to find one truly poor in spirit? ... Ah! do let us stay very far from all that glitters. Let us love our littleness, love to feel nothing, then we shall be poor in spirit and Jesus will come for us far off as we are and transform us in love's flame.[9]

St Thérèse understood with rare clarity (and in this she is a disciple of St John of the Cross) the profound, divine reality of poverty of spirit and humility. Alas, these blessed words become cliches and spiritual people too readily think that they know what the words mean and possess them. They are debased to something that 'glitters', affording self-satisfaction.

> I have always said to God: 'O my God, I really want to listen to You. I beg You to answer me when I say humbly: "What is truth?" Make me see things as they really are. Let nothing cause me to be deceived.'[10]

Somewhere along the line, we find the truth about ourselves too hard to bear. There is no way to truth save through the 'narrow gate', the resistant door that yields not one wit to arrogance, or any form of ego-seeking. Many people are genuinely very good and are excellent in community and yet, in all sorts of subtle ways, they reveal to the discerning eye of one who, to some extent at least, tries to live in the truth, that, in spite of a genuine desire for God, the dominant motive of their lives is the spiritual enhancement of the self. Few escape this danger altogether, though some are much more infected than others. Occasionally we have an arch example. Such a one is what we mean by a *poseur* and is totally unsuitable for the office of novice mistress. A postulant or novice who has even an ordinary degree of insight, will detect lack of authenticity and fail to be impressed. But harm can accrue to the young, romantically minded candidate. However, if the prioress herself is true and the community understands to some degree what is, in fact, the deep heart of our charism, namely, to remain exposed in naked poverty to the purifying, transforming love of God, there is little likelihood of such a one being appointed. Not infrequently, a *poseur* has considerable natural gifts of intelligence and charm, and maybe a flair for the poetic, so that she dazzles the naive. Lacking self-knowledge, failing to look at and accept her darker emotions and true motivation, she will not know how to lead her charges in the way of truth and cannot but foster spiritual fantasy. Moreover, consciously or unconsciously, she will be seeking their admiration and affection, whereas a novice mistress must resolutely confront this natural desire and renounce it completely. Her sole aim must be the good of those she directs.

True mysticism has everything to do with reality and the mistress must courageously stand within her own truth, speak, teach and counsel from it, never pretending to be more than she is, to know more than she does. As already said, she needs a great deal of self-knowledge and readiness for further revelations of her own weakness, compulsions and lack of truth, without ever being discouraged, but entrusting herself and the office she holds to God's loving care. Almost a necessity for her is someone to whom she can confide her own weaknesses, uncertainties, and struggles, as this is one of the best ways of ensuring growth in self-knowledge, purity of heart, and confidence in God, which will enable her, no matter how abashed she feels at her ignorance and sinfulness, never to abdicate her authority. No matter how painfully self-aware she is, when dealing with her novices all reflection on self must be laid aside. It is to *them* she must listen, *them* she must address. Her whole attention must be on their condition and needs, disregarding entirely her own emotions of self-distrust, diffidence, anxiety, or whatever they may be.

God is faithful. As religious we hand ourselves over to this fidelity. Religious life is one huge act of trust. Living faithful to a Rule, abandoning self-direction and choice, submitting for love of God to the authority of the Rule and of the superiors, we can confidently assume that, if we do our very best, God will see to it that we receive – and give – the nourishment all need. Objectively speaking, the food offered may be poor in quality but, if humbly proffered and humbly received, we can be sure that, passing through divine hands, it is transformed into rich food. Humility and trust are needed both by those whose duty it is to provide the food, and by those who are to be fed. But 'the Sister chosen for this office should not be negligent or remiss, since it is a question of forming souls in whom the Lord makes His abode.'[11] Each one is different, so very different, and she must lovingly study each one, must really dedicate herself, with all her mind and heart to her formation.

Formation

Every formal grouping of Carmels has its *ratio*, a comprehensive programme, covering the manifold aspects of the formation of Teresian Carmelite nuns. There is no need to plough over that well-worked field. Enough has been said already of the importance of intellectual formation and the whole content of this book is on the formation of a

Carmelite, so none of it will be repeated here. The novice mistress can, and should, engage others to work with the novices at theology, biblical studies and liturgy, though herself maintaining the overall organisation and responsibility. It is wise to control the novices' reading for they must learn to read well and care must be taken that the hour daily assigned to reading, is used to advantage. When all is said and done, the greater part of the sisters' intellectual formation is effected by themselves throughout the course of their lives. What we have to do is to ensure that they acquire a taste for solid reading, if they lack it, and cultivate a disciplined mind. Certainly we are advocating a sustained intellectual effort, but the aim is not an academic one, is not the mere acquisition of knowledge, but simply, to learn all we can about the Beloved whom we encounter, so personally, so deeply, in solitary prayer. Such 'learning about' is essential for those who are called to be contemplatives, whose whole being is to be orientated, as consciously as possible, to God all day long.

Besides the transmission of the charism, 'the forming of souls in whom God make His abode' is the special field of the mistress: in other words, formation in prayer and all that relates most intimately to prayer. Teresa enjoined that each of the novices was to give the mistress each day

> an account of her prayer, how she had got on with the Mystery she was contemplating, what fruit she derived from it.[12]

Of course, this ordinance cannot be taken literally, but it clearly shows that the foundress expected the mistress to be the spiritual teacher, guide and director of the novices. Anyone who 'breezes in' on a young sister's relationship with Our Lord, is not fit for the office and it is good to feel diffident and to tread softly, very softly. However, too easily this particular aspect of formation can be neglected through shyness and diffidence. We are ready enough to transmit objectively the teaching of our saints on prayer, but fall back on the slogan that only the Holy Spirit can teach prayer; so, a novice's prayer can be left to look after itself.

No! The novice mistress must realise that she herself is one of the principal means whereby the Holy Spirit will teach and guide. It is her sacred duty to enter this area and she owes it to her charges to do so. The sisters have come to Carmel precisely to learn from the cumulative wisdom of Carmel how to grow in union with God through prayer. We can be confident that the Holy Spirit will be present and active where there is love, humility and poverty of spirit. Even a maturer entrant who has prayed for many years – and the temptation to leave her alone is all the greater – must not be denied the benefits of what Carmel has to offer in the way of the deeper things. It will soon become obvious if this postulant is merely seeking a spiritual home where she can more freely give herself up to *her* prayer, her own understanding of 'what it is all about', or whether grace has revealed to her, however inchoately, that something is lacking and she dimly perceives depths of selfishness that must be purged, and a yearning potential that, for her, can be realised to the full only through the ascesis of Carmel. We must not deny her this ascesis, and the humble receiving of instruction and direction from the one appointed, regardless of who she is, is very much part of this.

She is to teach them how to act in times of sweetness and spiritual aridity and how to break their will even in small things.[13]

The integration and maturation of the emotions, indispensable for genuine contemplation, though a lifelong endeavour, must receive special attention in the novitiate. This is not always appreciated as it should be. To begin with, the 'desert' aspect of Carmel – enclosure, the lack of diversion and supportive comforts, silence, aloneness – inevitably means that self-awareness sharpens and states of feeling are acutely experienced. They invade the consciousness, clamouring for attention and outlet. Moreover, emotions, hitherto unrecognised and unclaimed, emerge to confuse and upset. Sooner or later, a postulant or novice will be thrown off balance, be bewildered, distressed, tempted, one more severely than another, but no one will escape nor is it desirable that she should. The more the prioress, novice mistress and the community as a whole, understand this process, the more will they automatically provide the atmosphere and environment where the neophyte can more easily be led to understand what is happening, and accept that, contrary to the messages she is giving to herself, it is pure grace, the work of Divine Love. God is taking her at her word and the barricades which she had erected to preserve her frightened little self from life's assaults, the *persona* she had adopted by which to charm and impress others, in order to be liked and to get on in the world, are being demolished. The Beloved wants her to find her real, unshakeable value, her preciousness, in his love for her. The mistress must tell her this over and over again in one way or another. The more she herself is immersed in this experience, the more she is likely to convince, comfort and set the novice free to find the Beloved in the mysterious depths of the mystery which is herself. She must watch that the novice does not fall back on repressing emotions but should encourage her to recognise them, admit them and suffer them in so far as they are troublesome and painful; accept them, but not live in them, not foster them.

Each one must, through meditation, good reading, prayer and the instructions she receives, form strong principles and motives that will stand firm no matter what the emotional tempest. How often we see the opposite! An emotional crisis arises and principles go to the wind for the time being: authority, obedience, fidelity to prayer. The emotions take over. The mistress must do all she possibly can to help a novice to see the importance of winning mastery of her emotional life. Without it she cannot become a real woman, who is dependable, makes fair judgments of people and events, is loving: that is, she is outside herself, concerned with others, with what is right, with what is for God's honour.

The mistress has to steer with extreme care. On the one hand, she must afford her charges the comfort and support they need in times of real affliction. On the other, her aim must be to lead them into solitude. To become contemplative they must learn to live alone. One important aspect of this is the ability to suffer in silence, to 'sink' beneath emotional pain and accustom themselves to find their comfort and support in Our Lord. If the mistress is always at hand to dry their tears and alleviate their pain (and who would not *want* to do this?) novices will never find him, never discover the depth within.

When all human, all creaturely solace is absent, there is no alternative if a sister is to survive in Carmel, but to 'go right down' to her foundation, to her deepest meaning and, in the pain and darkness, receive (maybe undetected by herself) the courage she needs and 'my peace' that the 'world' cannot give.

A common phenomenon of the novitiate period is the upsurge of emotional love for the mistress, the prioress or some member of the community. It can take the novice herself by surprise and cause her a lot of distress and pain. The feeling can be very intense. The best thing, when it is detected, is to bring it into the open but in such a way that the 'sufferer' – for she is suffering – feels not in the least demeaned. Her counsellor, even if she is the object of the love, must convey her respect and her understanding. Anything approaching a derisive 'shove off' is wrong and harmful. If the one counselling has herself experienced such an emotional involvement, she will know how painful it is and how easily it produces a sense of guilt. The novice can be reassured that what is happening to her is a blessing, an opportunity to confront emotional and sexual immaturities of which she was unaware, and that could have remained unresolved for the rest of her life. Here is her chance for further growth into mature womanhood. The counsellor must remain scrupulously objective and 'in the truth', never allowing the novice to think that her love is returned in a similar fashion. This is what the novice is yearning for but her overtures must be gently resisted. Such a return, far from satisfying her, would increase her unhappiness. Let her be quite confident that she is loved and will continue to be loved, that she has a loyal friend. As the years go by, provided that now she sacrifices her craving for the sort of response she wants, she will find that supportive, quietly satisfying friendships will develop.

However, now, all between the two of them must be wholly appropriate to the relationship of novice mistress (or prioress) to novice. The situation will be overly difficult if the novice has no companion. It probably is better that the one who is the object of the affection remain 'ignorant' and another be trusted with this delicate task. Much depends on how well it is handled. Hopefully, this frank, sympathetic yet firm approach will prove of great benefit. If the novice rejects it and in all sort of ways makes emotional demands, then she is proved unfit for the life.

The mistress must tirelessly teach that, as Christians, and supremely as Carmelite Christians, we must live by faith and not by feeling, by what we know by faith is truth. The novices must be taught to be attentive, reflective and to avoid 'drifting', heedlessness. This means that all the time, literally all the time, they should know what they are doing and why they are doing it. Frequently they should actually formulate these questions to themselves. Likewise, they should question themselves very seriously, searchingly, deeply: What do I *really* want? By 'want', is not meant a mere emotion or liking. Rather, it refers to the deepest reaching out of our inmost heart when it confronts life's meaning. What do I want to want? What am I, at my deepest level, *really* looking for? All this is to help them to live deeply, alone before God, totally responsible for their own lives, for the choices they make day by day. Just as emotional dependency is ruled out, so is the sloughing off of responsibility on to the prioress or novice mistress.

The incontrovertible truth that Jesus' friends live by faith and not by feeling, must above all, govern prayer. When she is assured that a novice is doing her best, the mistress must painstakingly repeat over and over again, that she, the worried novice, cannot assess her prayer by how she feels about it. To do so is lack of faith. Let her reflect on what Jesus shows us of God and then ask how such a God could fail her or in any way be displeased by her humble effort. Rather, he is grateful to her as she allows him to purify her of self-seeking in prayer, as he intends to communicate his own divine Self to her. She must be glad, not sad and find peace in aridity, in 'nothing happening'. This lesson is not easily learned as everyone knows!

To conclude on a note of realism: there is no such thing as the perfect novice mistress, no such thing as flawless direction. All that is asked of us is to give our very best to those who wish to join us. The results we leave to God.

CHAPTER THIRTEEN

The Prioress

The first thing I require is for you to have a Prior, one of yourselves, who is to be chosen for the office by common consent, or
that of the greater or maturer part of you. Each of the others must
promise him obedience – of which, once he has promised, he must
try to make his deeds the true reflection.[1]

An inalienable element in the Teresian charism is the government of the community by one person, as the Rule
ordains. We are not, and cannot be a democracy. To
undercut this 'first thing' required, to diminish the
authority of this one person, to insist on greater 'power
sharing' is to deprive ourselves of one of the principle
instruments God uses by which we can die to self, to ego-
desire, to ego-control, and come to the impoverishment,
the spiritual nakedness that are the reverse side of being
filled with the fullness of God.

Would that I could convince spiritual persons that the road to God
consists . . . only in the one thing that is needful, which is the ability to deny oneself truly, according to that which is without and
that which is within.[2]

St Teresa held unquestioningly to this first point of the
Rule. Obedience to the prioress holds an important place

in her teaching on asceticism. However, Carmelite superiors are not imposed from without; the sisters themselves choose whom they want. The prioress is to be 'one of yourselves' and this indicates far more than that she is a member of the community. It implies an attitude of mind, a particular approach to authority, both on the part of the one who holds it, and on those who choose to be subject to it. Picked from among themselves, it is their wish that she exercises authority for the good of all, but all the while, in herself she remains simply, 'one of yourselves'. Understood as it ought to be, this rules out any *mystique* surrounding the person and office, an unreality that can corrupt the prioress herself and all but negate the ascetic value of obedience.

When appraising Teresa's constitutions we must bear in mind that the Reform was only twenty years old when she died, and that gave hardly adequate time for every item to be thoroughly tested. What is more, because all her writings, and this includes her Constitutions, rise out of her own long experience of herself, of other people and of life in religious houses, inconsistencies are not lacking, and being the woman she was, she indulges here and there, in idealistic flourishes that we cannot take seriously still less apply literally. Therefore, it is not easy to form a clear idea of the sort of superior Teresa wanted her prioresses to be. The image she projects shifts. In conformity with the Rule she assigns to a prioress wide powers. The nature of a life tending to eremiticism, demands that the manifold decisions and arrangements that the day to day life of a community involves, are in the hands of one person and of officials who, their specific, limited independent responsibilities apart, function in subordination to her.

The principal duty of the prioress is to

> ... take great care in everything about the observance of the rule and constitutions, to look after the integrity of the enclosure of the house, to observe how the offices are carried out, and to see that both spiritual and temporal needs are provided for.[3]

A service indeed but one that involves the exercise of wide powers. This aspect of the office does not demand great spirituality and discernment. Rather, it calls for a lot of common sense, intelligence and a gift for organisation. But Teresa seems to expect more. The prioress is to be not merely a caretaker and manageress; but a matriarch, the spiritual leader and director of the community.

> All the Sisters should give the prioress a monthly account of how they have done in prayer, of how the Lord is leading them, for His Majesty will give her light so that if they are not proceeding well she might guide them.[4]

This implies that she is a woman of much spirituality and capable of guiding all the members of her community, and this is surely unrealistic. The *Book of the Foundations*, but above all her letters (which, of course, were never intended for publication) give us an idea of the trouble Teresa had in finding suitable prioresses for her foundations, and the 'headache' some of them were to her with their incompetence and follies. The idealism she expresses in her Constitutions is counter balanced by some confidential disclosures in her letters. But there is a further incongruity in that the sisters were expected to give the prioress their confidence in spiritual matters and yet, at the end of three years this particular person ceases to be prioress. Did Teresa really expect that the nuns would then transfer the spiritual intimacy to her successor? Have we not to admit that in this instance, as in others, the saint did not always think matters through?

At the beginning of the Reform, Teresa herself was prioress and, of course, the inspiration, spiritual guide and mother of the little community. In the case of the first few foundations she had capable women at hand and, in any case, kept in close touch with the sisters of the convents, remaining their spiritual mother and guide. It was when foundations multiplied that the problem arose, a problem not reflected in her legislation. Her relief was enormous when Father Gratian became Provincial and therefore the superior of the nuns. Travelling round, visiting the communities, he could act as her representative, well briefed, of course! She had no doubt that the welfare of a community depended to a great extent on the prioress: 'There may be many saintly women who are not fitted to be prioresses, and any such must be removed quickly'. If the demoted one is offended then her unfitness is clearer than ever![5]

And:

> It is impossible that all nuns who are elected as prioresses can have the gifts necessary for that office, and whenever such a person is found wanting in them she must be removed during her first year. For in a single year she can do little harm; but if she holds office for three, she may ruin the convent by allowing imperfections to become habitual.[6]

Even if the Provincial believes her to be a saint he must not hesitate to remove her from office. Teresa highly commends some prioresses for the way they govern and the consequent peace of their communities in contrast to the turmoil in those lacking good leadership. In general, when it came to choosing a prioress, Teresa preferred intelligence and common sense to saintliness, and the sort of person she describes in the *Way*:

> When an intelligent person begins to grow fond of what is good, she clings to it manfully, for she sees that it is the best thing for her; this course may not bring her great spirituality, but it will help her to give profitable advice, and to make herself useful in many ways, without being a trouble to anybody.[7]

Centuries have passed since Teresa penned her ideals and her worries about the governance of her monasteries. What evolved and was handed down was a decidedly autocratic form of government, and an unhealthy 'spiritualising' of the superior. The governance may have been and often was, maternal and kindly, but authoritarian nevertheless and only unusual spiritual maturity and clear-headedness could enable a prioress to disengage herself entirely from the mystical cocoon in which the community as a whole chose to swaddle her. A cocoon can be safe and comfortable! Governing a community 'old style' was simpler and easier whatever its human and spiritual drawbacks. The way of life itself was minutely patterned and uniform, and more or less unchanging. Every office had a book of instructions, handed down from one generation to the next, rich in detail, as to how the office was to be run. There was no room for innovation or creativity. In many ways, the office of prioress too was stereotyped. The newly-elected had seen for herself the pattern to be followed, observed how a prioress behaved and what she did.

A strange metamorphosis took place. Before the election, the now Mother X was simply Sister X with her qualities and also her limitations. After her installation she suddenly acquired a new 'face'. She was now 'Our Mother', a sacred person, endowed with spirituality and discernment, whom the Holy Spirit constantly guided. No one need worry. Everything could safely be left to our mother. She was not to be questioned, still less criticised. Inward veneration was expressed and fostered outwardly. One stepped aside and bowed when she passed, knelt to speak to her, kissed the ground at the slightest rebuke, kissed her hand or scapular. An impartial observer might well wonder at the mysterious need which induced these women positively to *want* to surround their prioress with such a *mystique*. Faults that in an ordinary member of the community would not be tolerated, in her were simply non-existent. The sisters simply did not want to see weaknesses and flaws in their head.

> O what poisonous praises I've seen served up to Mother Prioress. How necessary that the person be detached from herself if she is not to be damaged.[8]

But how easily the poor creature fell victim to the role! And what immaturity and unreality was fostered in the community! Generalisations are always unfair and dangerous and many who knew the 'old style', or maybe themselves held office 'old style', might justifiably feel outraged. But there are others who will recognise only too clearly the truth within these generalisations, notwithstanding the genuine affection with which they still hold their prioresses of bygone days. Moreover, there were always a few, possibly very few, in a community, who inwardly stood aloof from this 'cult'. Theirs was a difficult course to steer: on the one hand refusing to 'kow-tow' and yet at the same time remaining respectful, complying with the outward customs, always obedient and generously understanding the difficulties of the one in office. We have a wonderful example of such integrity in Thérèse.

Our concern is with our own times. Throughout the Church, the model of authority has changed and, in principle at least, we are closer to the Gospel. Our eyes are set on Jesus. There are unplumbable depths in the biblical image of the 'servant'. Jesus, our Master, is among us as one who serves and how manifest, how incessant, how unsparing of himself was his service: preaching, healing, feeding, consoling to his total Self-expenditure on the cross. Behind our lowly Lord and Servant Jesus, we discern the Father, giving us all he has to give, sparing nothing, not even his own son. Who sees me, sees the Father. Jesus in all things does what he sees the Father doing. The mystery of the Suffering Servant! Be perfect as your heavenly Father is perfect.

How can anyone, taking up office with her eyes fixed on Jesus, look for any self-advantage in the honour done to her? Devout people speak eloquently of servanthood and, to some extent, try to practise it, but nowhere is delusion easier. Yes, we fervently and somewhat condescendingly engage to serve others, as a favour, but that is not enough. We have to *become a servant,* to be reckoned as one and treated as one. That is quite a different matter! All that was said earlier of the need for the novice mistress to stand resolutely in her own truth, in her poverty, opening herself to ever deeper self-knowledge and, trustfully, courageously, drawing it into herself, applies even more to a prioress. Consciously she must face the fact that the office holds subtle temptations for her. If she imagines herself immune, she is deceiving herself and the only safe way is to resolve over and over again to seek herself in nothing: no little liberties and exemptions, no angling for appreciation, sympathy and affection, no diversions that are not allowed to others, no shirking of contradictions and criticisms, no avoiding painful encounters in which her self-esteem is likely to be wounded. Over and over again she has to tell herself that her feelings, her convenience, her weariness and aching heart, her likes and dislikes are quite unimportant. 'A Mother Prioress', the young Thérèse of Lisieux told her sister, 'must always allow others to believe she is without suffering.'[9] And another word of her loving wisdom:

> What draws down God's lights and helps upon us when we are guiding and consoling souls is not telling of our own troubles in order to receive consolation, besides, this is not real consolation, it excites rather than calms us down.[10]

The prioress is allowed to have only one focus, the true good of others. Such self-renunciation is not achieved all at once if ever. Who will not fall time and time again? What matters is consciously to hold to this aim and work towards it, standing shamed before its unattained beauty, tirelessly praying to be shown the truth, to see things as they really are, and that includes oneself. Of course, different temperaments will have different areas of battle, feeling the force of different temptations. How easy to protect one's vulnerability behind the role, to resort to self-assertion in the name of authority, or, contrariwise, to manipulate the emotions of the community by touching expressions of weakness and inadequacy, making it only too obvious that one is wounded, over-tired, discouraged. Sisters would have to be hard-hearted (unless of course they see through the ploy) to make demands on such a one, or in any way pose a 'threat'. What self-knowledge is needed in the office! What determination not to savour one morsel of the poisonous food that some are sure to offer!

No one person has all the qualities that go to make the ideal prioress, though undoubtedly some one will have more than others. Naturally, we would want a gifted person but our sphere of choice is severely limited. Unless a gifted prioress, one who is a born leader, truly embraces the searching asceticism outlined above, she can do much harm even in what appears success. Without great asceticism, the office will merely be an outlet for her gifts of creativity, scope for her energies and the sisters will be used to minister to her egotism. Imperceptibly perhaps, she acquires an emotional centrality and becomes too dominant in the community consciousness. We are back then with the same disadvantages that the 'old style' propagated. Of course, this need not be so. A gifted person, alive to the dangers to herself as well as to her community, embracing servanthood with all her heart, will not merely neutralise the possible dangers but use her gifts to help the sisters to mature, gain experience and be independent of her.

As already suggested, a person of ordinary ability can make an excellent prioress, a far better one than an unpurified gifted sister. If she is humble and sensible, she will not hesitate to make full use of others' gifts to complement her own and enrich the community. A lot depends on the community as to whether a sister becomes a good prioress or not. She can be 'spoiled' by flattery and false sympathy but equally hamstrung by constant criticism, a readiness to find fault, to harass and question. When the community is non-patterned and of independent mind, open to dialogue and discussion there can be a temptation on the part of a diffident prioress to abdicate her authority on behalf of the community. This she may not do. If sisters have a thorough grasp of the theology of religious authority and obedience as they ought to have, and if they accept this means of sanctification with their whole heart, their attitude will make it easy for the prioress to exercise her authority.

On the one hand there will be no over-dependence, no 'cult', no servile acquiescence and, on the other hand, no insensitive criticism that can drive an inexperienced prioress, struggling to do her best, to become defensive and even resort to 'playing the role'. That would be a great pity. After all, nice, good people are noted for treating their servants with consideration and kindness! Shown affection, respect and given full cooperation, she will gain experience and her gifts will develop for the benefit of all. If she loves the charism and resolutely maintains the structure, makes firm decisions, organises everything well, and treats the sisters with courtesy and respect, she will be doing a great work. One of the very best she can offer – and nothing is more potent in raising up a slack community – is to show her esteem for the contemplative life by her own fidelity to all the hours set aside for prayer, so much so that, if she is missing, the community know that there is an unavoidable reason. A temptation for some prioresses is to grow careless, to prolong conversations, business meetings, parlours when there is no necessity. For some natures, all this is far more interesting and rewarding than difficult hours of prayer. There can be heartening feedback too in an admiration which perhaps her own community fail to show her. Yet if her heart is set on God as it surely must be if she is to be faithful to her vocation, all this worldliness will be resisted. Strong motivation will lead her to make sure that everything is so arranged and that employees, business people and others, understand very well that Carmelites are not free, that they have a strict timetable to adhere to. Normally this integrity wins their respect. Where there is a will there is a way! If a prioress finds herself without time for prayer, is frequently absent from community acts, she should ask herself if she is delegating sufficiently or is she wanting a finger in every pie, taking too much on herself instead of handing over to others what can be handed over to others? The more she delegates the better for her community and for herself. Of course, it is her duty to ensure that the offices are run in accordance with the values of Carmel and this will be most important wherever there is contact with outside. But when reasonably assured of that, then the more she trusts others, the greater competence and sense of responsibility they will acquire and she will have time for what is specifically her area: reading and reflecting on the meaning of Carmel, thinking about what is best for each and all, planning, organising, being available for the sisters, giving full time to prayer and, last but not least, taking a fair share of the ordinary domestic chores 'so that she might give good example to all'.[11]

She [the prioress] should strive to be loved so that she may be obeyed.[12]

More importantly, the prioress must strive to show herself trustworthy for who would not love a truly trustworthy person? What are the characteristics of such a trustworthiness? A person who is reliable, predictable, can be depended upon, is not blown about by her own emotions, likes and dislikes. She never plays false, favourable one moment, judgmental the next, saying one thing to your face and another behind your back. She knows how to keep herself out of the line of vision and judge impartially. You can count on her being devoted to your interest and that your good matters more than her prestige, advantage, convenience; that her good will is stable, not here today and gone tomorrow. When she herself is under pressure, censure or personal suffering, she will still remain just, kind and caring. You know that she means what she says and says what she means and is totally devoid of treachery. She can be trusted to keep your confidences and your reputation is safe with her. What are loving sentiments and any number of expressions of maternal tenderness compared with such trustworthiness, for which we all must strive but none more so than a prioress?

The more unobtrusive the servant-prioress becomes the better. Trusting her community, leaving each sister to her own field of responsibility, she can remain a quiet, prayerful presence, unconsciously exuding peace and security as she herself grows in love.

Notes

PREFACE: *by the Reverend Roger Spencer*

1. Cf. Jn 8:55.
2. *Perfectae Caritatis* 7.

CHAPTER ONE: *Great Desires*

1. E. Allison Peers (translator and editor), *The Way of Perfection*, chapter 21, in *The Complete Works of St Teresa of Jesus*. London: Sheed & Ward, 1946.
2. Ibid., chapter 8.
3. Ibid., chapter 13.
4. Peers, *Primitive Constitutions*, p. 24.
5. Peers, *The Way of Perfection*, chapter 1.
6. Ibid., chapter 40.
7. Ibid., chapter 13.
8. Peers, 'The Life', p. 32.
9. Ibid., chapter 45.
10. Peers, *The Book of Foundations*, chapter 1.
11. Ibid.
12. Peers, *The Way of Perfection*, chapter 1.
13. Ibid., chapter 18.
14. Ibid.
15. Aquinas, St Thomas, *Summa Theologiae*, Q188, Art 6.
16. Peers, 'The Life', chapter 34.
17. *Perfectae Caritatis* 7.

18. David Lewis (translator), *The Spiritual Canticle of St John of the Cross*. London: Thomas Baker, 1909, stanza 28.
19. Peers, *The Way of Perfection*, chapter 13.

CHAPTER TWO: *The Source*

1. Peers, 'The Life', chapter 37.
2. Peers, *The Interior Castle*, Mansions 5, chapter 1.
3. Joachim Smet, O. Carm.: *The Carmelites*. Private publication 1975, p. 17.
4. I rely here on the research of Jodi Bilinkoff, *The Avila of St Teresa: Religious Reform in the Sixteenth Century*. Cornell University Press, Ithaca and London.
5. Peers, 'The Life', chapter 37.
6. Letter to Dona Luisa de la Cerda, 7 November 1571.
7. Peers, 'The Life', chapter 35.
8. Peers, *The Way of Perfection*, chapter 11.
9. For the early history of the Carmelite order, I rely on the authority of Bede Edwards, O.C.D., *The Rule of St Albert*. Private publication 1973, p. 83.
10. Peers, 'The Life', chapter 35.
11. Ibid.
12. Peers, *The Book of Foundations*, chapter 9.
13. Edwards, *The Rule of St Albert*, p. 1.
14. Smet, *The Carmelites*, Vol. 1, p. 22.
15. Peers, 'The Life', chapter 23.
16. Peers, *The Way of Perfection*, chapter 7.
17. Peers, 'The Life', chapter 17.
18. Peers, *The Way of Perfection*, chapter 7.
19. Peers, *The Interior Castle*, Mansions 6, chapter 7.

CHAPTER THREE: *The Return to the Source*

1. Peers, *The Interior Castle*, Mansions 5, chapter 1.
2. Peers, *The Spiritual Canticle*, stanza 28.
3. Peers, *The Way of Perfection*, chapter 4.
4. Cf. Weber, *Teresa of Avila and a Rhetoric of Femininity*, New Jersey,

NJ: Princeton University Press. This study offers background information and stimulating interpretations even though one finds oneself disagreeing with some of them and the conclusions drawn.

5. Bilinkoff, *The Avila of St Teresa*.
6. Peers, 'The Life', chapter 7.
7. Ibid., chapter 21.
8. Letter to Don Lorenzo de Cepeda, 23 December 1561.
9. Peers, 'The Life', chapter 35.
10. Peers, *The Way of Perfection*, chapter 10.
11. Lewis, *The Spiritual Canticle*, stanzas 28 and 29.
12. Peers, *The Book of Foundations*, chapter 30.
13. 1 Cor 12:4–8.
14. Peers, *The Way of Perfection*, chapter 10.
15. Ibid., chapter 13.
16. Ibid., chapter 32.
17. Peers, *The Book of Foundations*, chapter 31.

CHAPTER FOUR: *Life of Dedicated Love*

1. Peers, *The Way of Perfection*, chapter 1.
2. Peers, *The Book of Foundations*, chapter 5.
3. Edwards, *The Rule of St Albert*.

CHAPTER FIVE: *The Charism Embodied*

1. Peers, 'The Life', chapter 36.
2. Peers, *The Book of Foundations*, chapter 29.
3. R. W. Southern, *The Making of the Middle Ages*, London: Hutchinson, 1953, p. 156.
4. Letter to Don Diego de San Pedro de la Palma, August 1570.
5. Letter to Don Diego de San Pedro de la Palma, 27 May 1571
6. Letter to Mother Maria de San Jose, November 1576.

CHAPTER SIX: *Eremiticism in the Teresian Carmel*

1. Peers, *The Book of Foundations*, chapter 2.
2. Peers, *Primitive Constitutions*, number 8.

3. Ibid., number 7.
4. Peers, *The Book of Foundations*, chapter 5.
5. Peers, *The Way of Perfection*, chapter 13.
6. Peers, 'The Life', chapter 37.
7. Lewis, *The Spiritual Canticle*, chapter 28.

CHAPTER SEVEN: *The Observance of Enclosure*

1. Peers, *The Book of Foundations*, chapter 31.
2. Peers, *Primitive Constitutions*, number 15.
3. Peers, *The Way of Perfection*, chapter 41.
4. Mt 10:37.
5. Letter to Senor Garcia de San Pedro, September 1571.

CHAPTER EIGHT: *Friendship among the Sisters – I*

1. Peers, *The Way of Perfection*, chapter 4.
2. Peers, *Primitive Constitutions*, number 26.
3. Ibid.
4. Peers, *The Way of Perfection*, chapter 4.
5. Ibid., chapter 5.
6. Peers, *The Interior Castle*, Mansions 5, chapter 3.
7. Peers, *Primitive Constitutions*, number 7.
8. Peers, *The Way of Perfection*, chapter 4.
9. Ibid.
10. Ibid.
11. Peers, *The Way of Perfection*, chapter 6.
12. Ibid., chapter 7.
13. Ronald Knox (translator), *Autobiography of a Saint*, London: Harvill Press, chapter 36.
14. Letter to Mother Marie de Gonzague, 1896.
15. Peers, *The Interior Castle*, Mansions 5, chapter 3.
16. *Lumen Gentium*, c.3, no.26.

CHAPTER NINE: *Friendship among the Sisters – II*

1. Peers, *Primitive Constitutions*, number 31.

2. Ibid., number 41.
3. Ibid., number 40.
4. Smet, *The Carmelites*, Vol. 2, pp. 121–4.
5. Peers, *Primitive Constitutions*, number 39.
6. Ibid., number 18.
7. Ibid., number 29.
8. Ibid., number 27.
9. Ibid., number 30.
10. Ibid., number 37.

CHAPTER TEN: *Unoccupied Prayer*

1. Mk 10:26–7.
2. Mk 10:15.
3. Jn 5:17.
4. Lk 10:38–42.
5. Mk 14:4.
6. Jn 14:9.
7. E. Allison Peers (translator and editor), *The Dark Night of the Soul*, Book 2, chapter 25, in *The Complete Works of St John of the Cross*. London: Burns & Oates, 1935.
8. Peers, *Primitive Constitutions*, number 8.
9. Peers, *The Way of Perfection*, chapter 21.
10. Ibid., chapter 17.
11. Cf. Goodenough, *The Sacred Depths of Nature*, Oxford: Oxford University Press, 1998.
12. Peers, *The Book of Foundations*, chapter 5.
13. Precautions: the third against the world.
14. Phil 4:8.

CHAPTER ELEVEN: *Asceticism*

1. Letter to Lorenzo de Cepeda, December 1563.
2. Peers, *Primitive Constitutions*, number 59.
3. Peers, *The Way of Perfection*, chapter 3.
4. Ibid., chapter 15.
5. Ibid., chapter 10.

6. Ibid., chapter 11.
7. Ibid.
8. Peers, *Primitive Constitutions*, number 22.
9. Ibid., number 23.
10. Ibid.
11. Ibid., number 32.
12. Ibid., number 13.
13. Ibid., number 12.
14. Ibid., number 22.
15. Ibid., number 10.
16. Ps 113.

CHAPTER TWELVE: *Formation*

1. Letter to Don Gaspar de Villanueva, July 1577.
2. Rule and Constitutions of the Discalced Nuns, 1991, no. 203.
3. Letter to Provincial Ambrosio Mariano, October 1576.
4. *Primitive Constitutions*, number 21.
5. Letter to Mother Maria de San Jose.
6. Letter to Provincial Ambrosio Mariano, October 1576.
7. Letter to Mother Maria de San Jose, September 1596.
8. *Primitive Constitutions*, number 40.
9. Letter to Mother Maria de San Jose, September 1596.
10. John Clarke, O.C.D. (translator and editor) *The Yellow Notebook of St Thérèse of Lisieux: her last Conversations.* London: I.C.S. Publications.
11. *Primitive Constitutions*, number 40.
12. Ibid.
13. Ibid.

CHAPTER THIRTEEN: *The Prioress*

1. Edwards, *The Rule of St Albert.*
2. Ascent, Book 2 c.7.
3. Peers, *Primitive Constitutions*, number 34.
4. Ibid.
5. Visitation of Convents.

6. Ibid.

7. Peers, *The Way of Perfection*, chapter 14.

8. Clarke, *The Yellow Notebook*.

9. Ibid.

10. Ibid.

11. Peers, *Primitive Constitutions*, number 22.

12. Ibid., number 34.

Lightning Source UK Ltd.
Milton Keynes UK
UKOW04f0258200614

233742UK00007B/81/P

9 780722 014516